The Murder
of Abraham Lincoln

cloth: ISBN-10: 1-56163-425-5
ISBN-13: 978-1-56163-425-5
paperback: ISBN-10: 1-56163-426-3
ISBN-13: 978-1-56163-426-2
©2005 Rick Geary
Printed in China

5   4   3   2   1

Library of Congress Cataloging-in-Publication Data

Geary, Rick.
    The murder of Abraham Lincoln / Rick Geary.
        p. cm. -- (A treasury of Victorian murder)
    ISBN 1-56163-425-5 (alk. paper) -- ISBN 1-56163-426-3 (pbk.: alk. paper)
    1. Lincoln, Abraham, 1809-1865--Assassination--Pictorial works. 2. Booth, John Wilkes, 1838-1865--Pictorial works.
3. Lincoln, Abraham, 1809-1865--Assassination--Caricatures and cartoons. 4. Booth, John Wilkes, 1838-1865--
Caricatures and cartoons. I. Title.
E457.5.G43 2005

                                        2005041468

Comicslit is an imprint
and trademark of

NANTIER · BEALL · MINOUSTCHINE
Publishing inc.
new york

THE
MURDER
OF
ABRAHAM
LINCOLN

A CHRONICLE OF 62 DAYS IN THE
LIFE OF THE AMERICAN REPUBLIC—
MARCH 4 — MAY 4, 1865

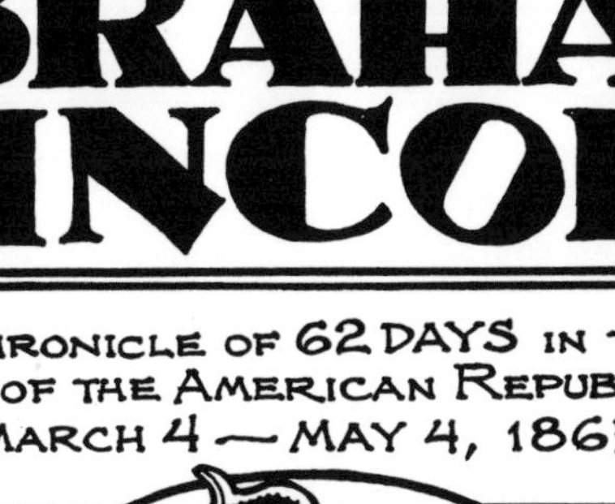

WRITTEN AND ILLUSTRATED BY
RICK GEARY

Also available by Geary:
A Treasury of Victorian Murder:
Vol. 1: pb.: $8.95
Vol. 2: Jack The Ripper, pb.: $7.95, hc.: $15.95
Vol. 3: The Borden Tragedy, pb.: $8.95
Vol. 4: The Fatal Bullet, pb.: $8.95
Vol. 5: The Mystery of Mary Rogers, pb.: $8.95, hc.: $15.95
Vol. 6: The Beast of Chicago, pb.: $8.95, hc.: $15.95

We have over 200 titles, write for our color catalog:
NBM
555 8th Ave., Suite 1202,
New York, NY 10018
see our website at
www.nbmpublishing.com

Victorian
MURDER
COMPILED AND ILLUSTRATED BY

A Treasury of
Victorian Murder
JACK the RIPPER
by
RICK GEARY

A TREASURY OF VICTORIAN MURDER
The BEAST of CHICAGO
THE MURDEROUS CAREER OF
H. H. HOLMES
RICK GEARY
ComicsLit

The Mystery of
Mary Rogers
RICK GEARY

A TREASURY OF
VICTORIAN MURDER
The Borden Tragedy
Rick Geary

THE FATAL BULLET
THE ASSASSINATION OF PRESIDENT JAMES A. GARFIELD
RICK GEARY
ComicsLit

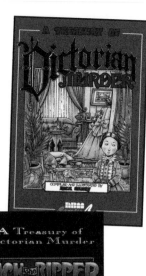

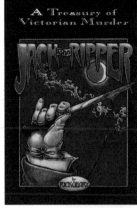

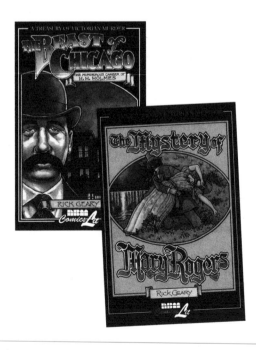

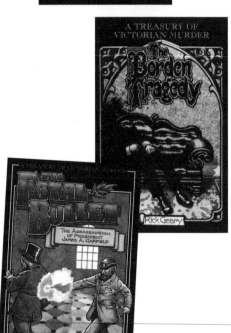

BIBLIOGRAPHY

Bishop, Jim, *The Day Lincoln was Shot*. (New York, Gramercy Books, 1955)

Donald, David Herbert, *Lincoln*. (New York, Simon & Schuster, 1995)

Donovan, Robert J., *The Assasins*. (New York, Popular Library, 1962)

Hanchett, William, *The Lincoln Murder Conspiracies*. (Chicago & Urbana, University of Illinois Press, 1986)

Kunhardt, Dorothy Meserve and Philip B. Kunhardt, Jr., *Twenty Days*. (New York, Castle Books, 1965)

Lewis, Lloyd, *Myths After Lincoln*. (New York, Harcourt, Brace, 1929)

Reck, W. Emerson, *A. Lincoln, His Last 24 Hours*. (Jefferson NC and London, McFarland & Co., Inc, 1987)

Steers, Edward, Jr., *Blood on the Moon*. (Lexington KY, The University Press of Kentucky, 2001)

Stern, Philip Van Doren, *The Man Who Killed Lincoln*. (New York, The Literary Guild of America, Inc, 1939)

Winkler, H. Donald, Lincoln and Booth. (Nashville TN, Cumberland House, 2003)

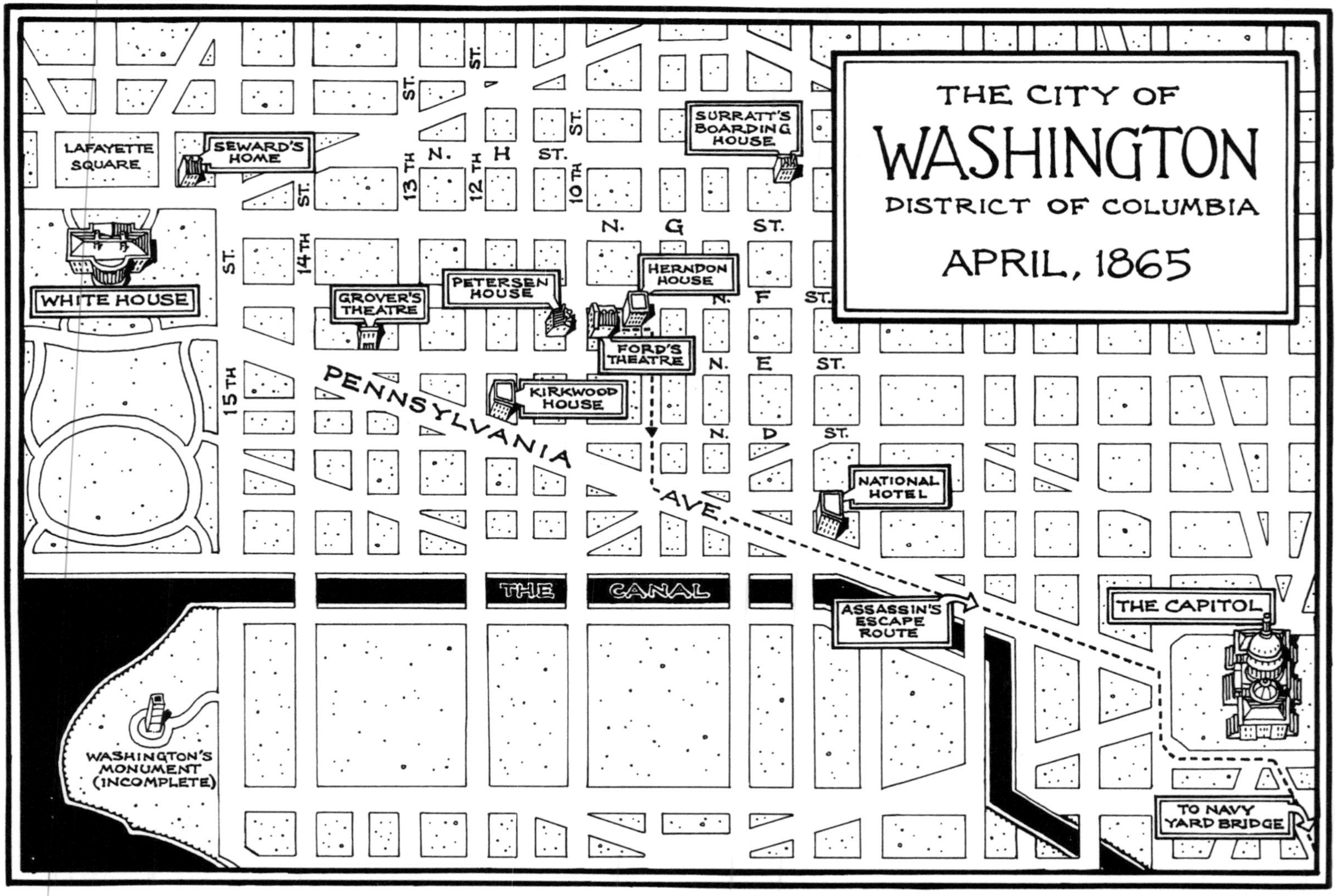
THE CITY OF
WASHINGTON
DISTRICT OF COLUMBIA
APRIL, 1865
LAFAYETTE SQUARE
SEWARD'S HOME
WHITE HOUSE
GROVER'S THEATRE
PETERSEN HOUSE
HERNDON HOUSE
FORD'S THEATRE
KIRKWOOD HOUSE
SURRATT'S BOARDING HOUSE
NATIONAL HOTEL
PENNSYLVANIA AVE.
15TH ST.
14TH ST.
13TH ST.
12TH ST.
10TH ST.
N. H ST.
N. G ST.
N. F ST.
N. E ST.
N. D ST.
THE CANAL
ASSASSIN'S ESCAPE ROUTE
THE CAPITOL
TO NAVY YARD BRIDGE
WASHINGTON'S MONUMENT (INCOMPLETE)

BIBLIOGRAPHY

Bishop, Jim, *The Day Lincoln was Shot.* (New York, Gramercy Books, 1955)

Donald, David Herbert, *Lincoln.* (New York, Simon & Schuster, 1995)

Donovan, Robert J., *The Assasins.* (New York, Popular Library, 1962)

Hanchett, William, *The Lincoln Murder Conspiracies.* (Chicago & Urbana, University of Illinois Press, 1986)

Kunhardt, Dorothy Meserve and Philip B. Kunhardt, Jr., *Twenty Days.* (New York, Castle Books, 1965)

Lewis, Lloyd, *Myths After Lincoln.* (New York, Harcourt, Brace, 1929)

Reck, W. Emerson, *A. Lincoln, His Last 24 Hours.* (Jefferson NC and London, McFarland & Co., Inc, 1987)

Steers, Edward, Jr., *Blood on the Moon.* (Lexington KY, The University Press of Kentucky, 2001)

Stern, Philip Van Doren, *The Man Who Killed Lincoln.* (New York, The Literary Guild of America, Inc, 1939)

Winkler, H. Donald, Lincoln and Booth. (Nashville TN, Cumberland House, 2003)

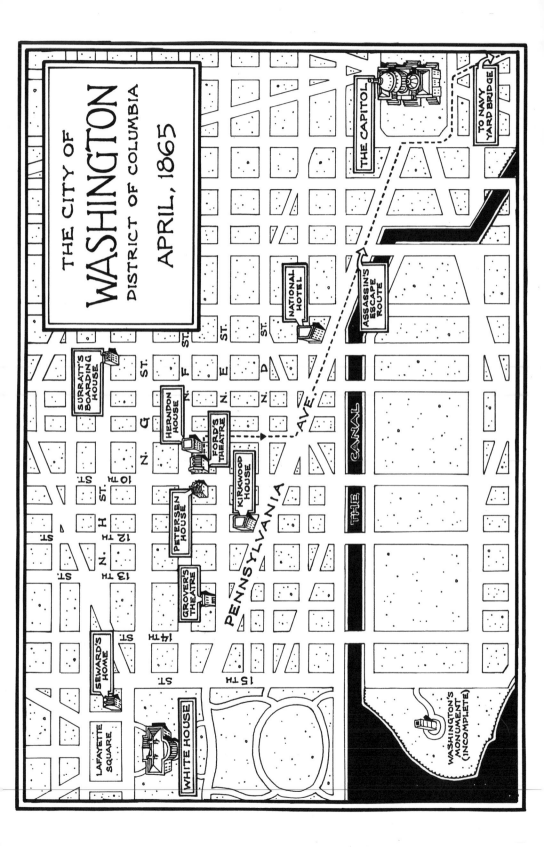

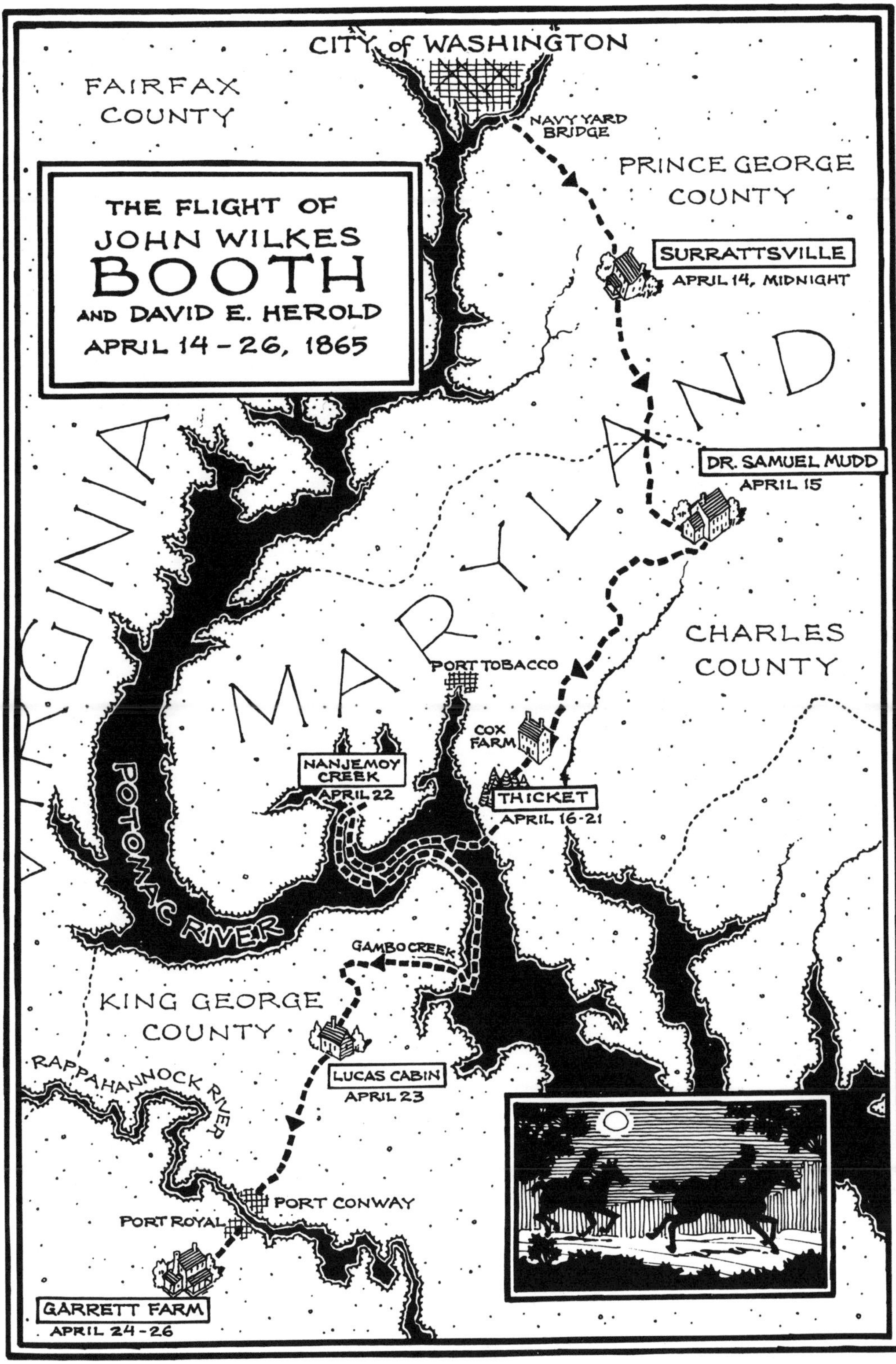
THE FLIGHT OF
JOHN WILKES
BOOTH
AND DAVID E. HEROLD
APRIL 14 - 26, 1865
CITY of WASHINGTON
FAIRFAX COUNTY
NAVY YARD BRIDGE
PRINCE GEORGE COUNTY
SURRATTSVILLE
APRIL 14, MIDNIGHT
MARYLAND
VIRGINIA
DR. SAMUEL MUDD
APRIL 15
CHARLES COUNTY
PORT TOBACCO
COX FARM
NANJEMOY CREEK
APRIL 22
THICKET
APRIL 16-21
POTOMAC RIVER
GAMBO CREEK
KING GEORGE COUNTY
LUCAS CABIN
APRIL 23
RAPPAHANNOCK RIVER
PORT CONWAY
PORT ROYAL
GARRETT FARM
APRIL 24-26

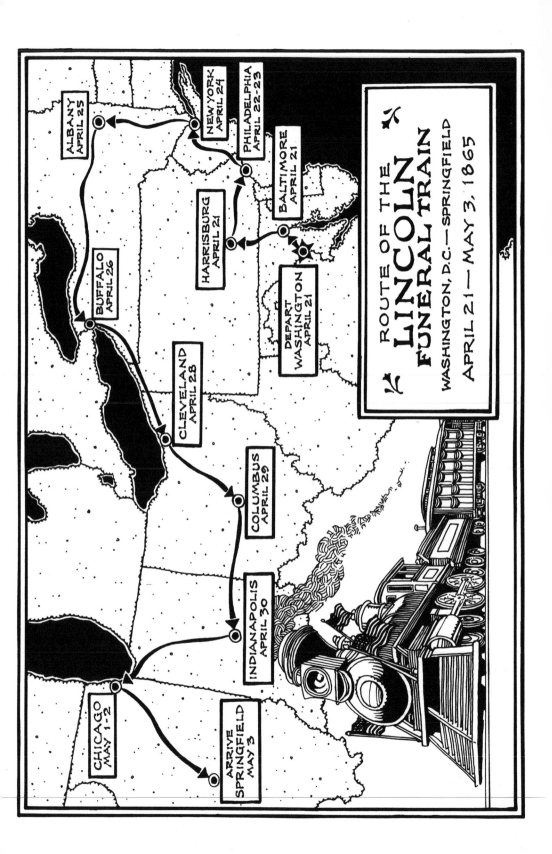

ROUTE OF THE
LINCOLN
FUNERAL TRAIN
WASHINGTON, D.C.—SPRINGFIELD
APRIL 21—MAY 3, 1865

DEPART WASHINGTON APRIL 21

BALTIMORE APRIL 21

HARRISBURG APRIL 21

PHILADELPHIA APRIL 22-23

NEW YORK APRIL 24

ALBANY APRIL 25

BUFFALO APRIL 26

CLEVELAND APRIL 28

COLUMBUS APRIL 29

INDIANAPOLIS APRIL 30

CHICAGO MAY 1-2

ARRIVE SPRINGFIELD MAY 3

PART I
THE PRESIDENT

THE WHITE HOUSE

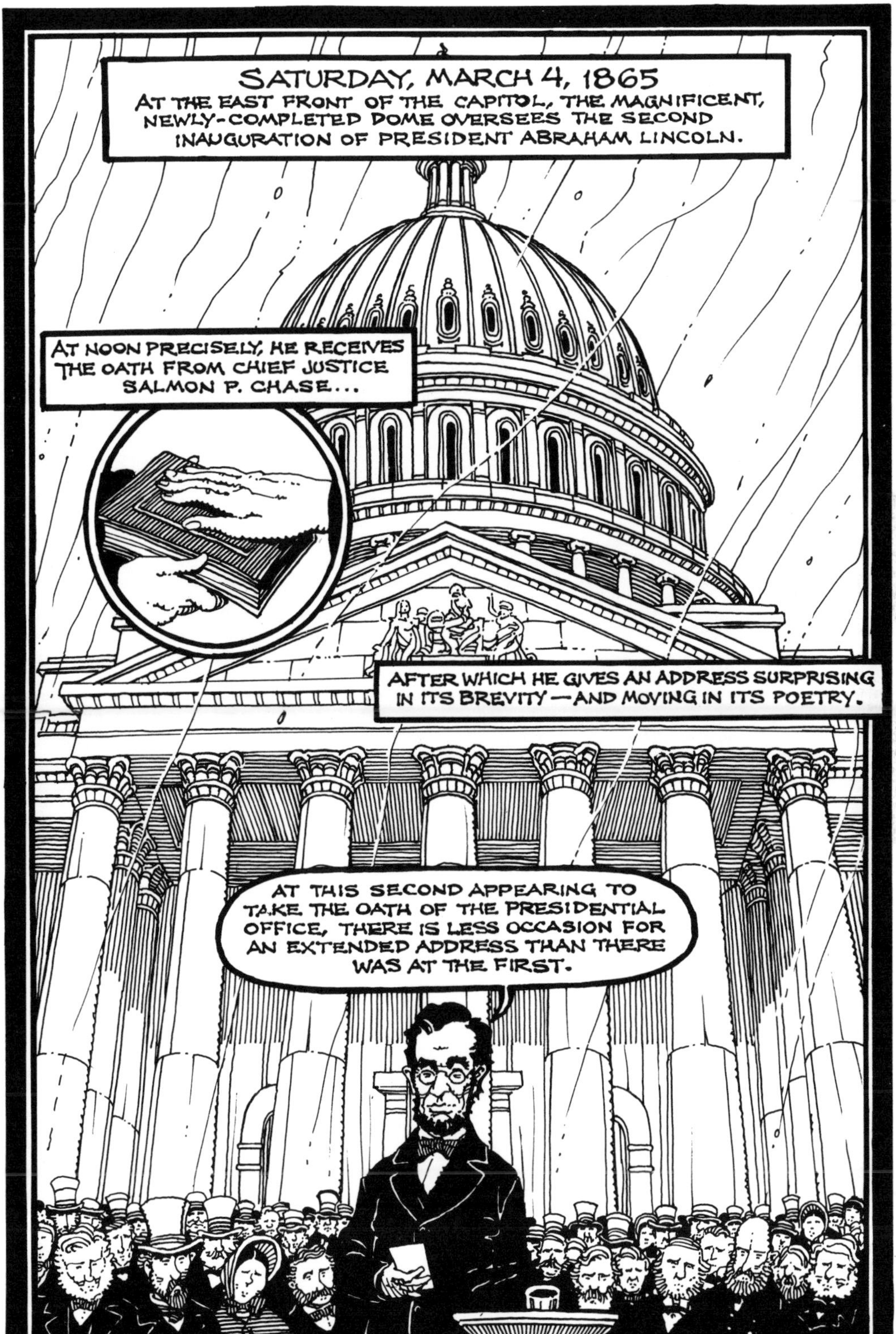
SATURDAY, MARCH 4, 1865
AT THE EAST FRONT OF THE CAPITOL, THE MAGNIFICENT, NEWLY-COMPLETED DOME OVERSEES THE SECOND INAUGURATION OF PRESIDENT ABRAHAM LINCOLN.
AT NOON PRECISELY, HE RECEIVES THE OATH FROM CHIEF JUSTICE SALMON P. CHASE...
AFTER WHICH HE GIVES AN ADDRESS SURPRISING IN ITS BREVITY—AND MOVING IN ITS POETRY.
AT THIS SECOND APPEARING TO TAKE THE OATH OF THE PRESIDENTIAL OFFICE, THERE IS LESS OCCASION FOR AN EXTENDED ADDRESS THAN THERE WAS AT THE FIRST.

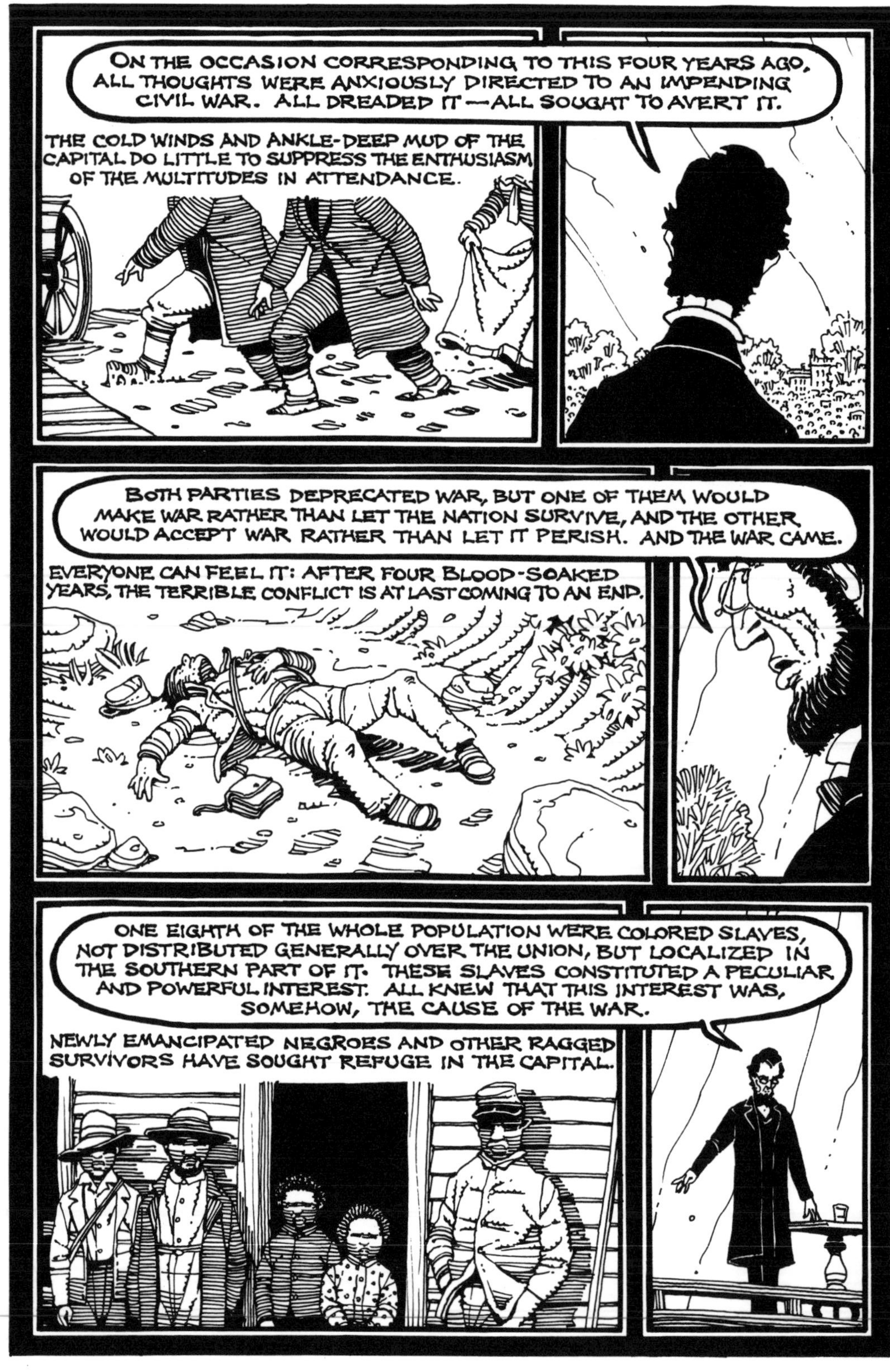
ON THE OCCASION CORRESPONDING TO THIS FOUR YEARS AGO, ALL THOUGHTS WERE ANXIOUSLY DIRECTED TO AN IMPENDING CIVIL WAR. ALL DREADED IT — ALL SOUGHT TO AVERT IT.
THE COLD WINDS AND ANKLE-DEEP MUD OF THE CAPITAL DO LITTLE TO SUPPRESS THE ENTHUSIASM OF THE MULTITUDES IN ATTENDANCE.
BOTH PARTIES DEPRECATED WAR, BUT ONE OF THEM WOULD MAKE WAR RATHER THAN LET THE NATION SURVIVE, AND THE OTHER WOULD ACCEPT WAR RATHER THAN LET IT PERISH. AND THE WAR CAME.
EVERYONE CAN FEEL IT: AFTER FOUR BLOOD-SOAKED YEARS, THE TERRIBLE CONFLICT IS AT LAST COMING TO AN END.
ONE EIGHTH OF THE WHOLE POPULATION WERE COLORED SLAVES, NOT DISTRIBUTED GENERALLY OVER THE UNION, BUT LOCALIZED IN THE SOUTHERN PART OF IT. THESE SLAVES CONSTITUTED A PECULIAR AND POWERFUL INTEREST. ALL KNEW THAT THIS INTEREST WAS, SOMEHOW, THE CAUSE OF THE WAR.
NEWLY EMANCIPATED NEGROES AND OTHER RAGGED SURVIVORS HAVE SOUGHT REFUGE IN THE CAPITAL.

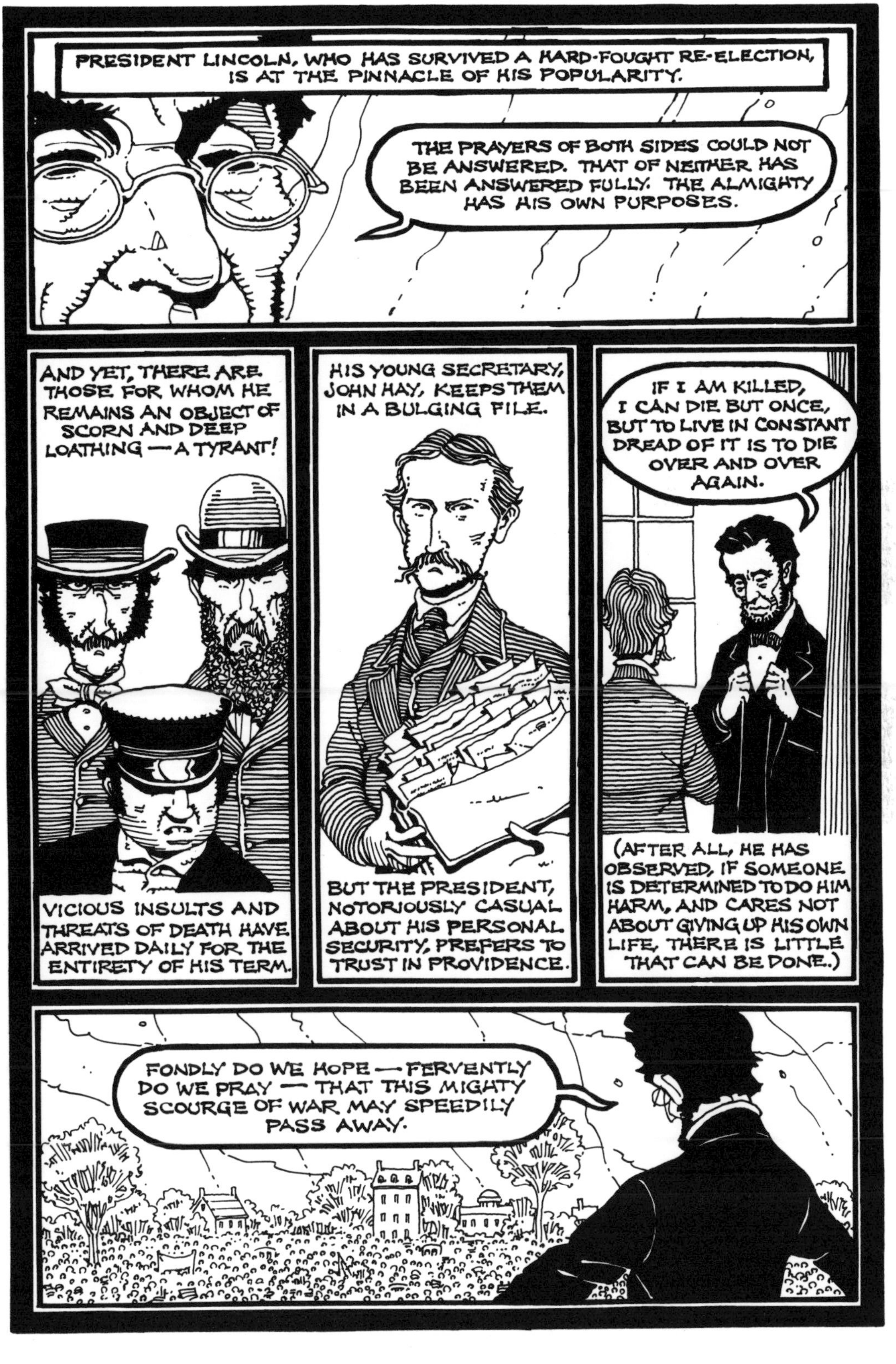
PRESIDENT LINCOLN, WHO HAS SURVIVED A HARD-FOUGHT RE-ELECTION, IS AT THE PINNACLE OF HIS POPULARITY.
THE PRAYERS OF BOTH SIDES COULD NOT BE ANSWERED. THAT OF NEITHER HAS BEEN ANSWERED FULLY. THE ALMIGHTY HAS HIS OWN PURPOSES.
AND YET, THERE ARE THOSE FOR WHOM HE REMAINS AN OBJECT OF SCORN AND DEEP LOATHING — A TYRANT!
VICIOUS INSULTS AND THREATS OF DEATH HAVE ARRIVED DAILY FOR THE ENTIRETY OF HIS TERM.
HIS YOUNG SECRETARY, JOHN HAY, KEEPS THEM IN A BULGING FILE.
BUT THE PRESIDENT, NOTORIOUSLY CASUAL ABOUT HIS PERSONAL SECURITY, PREFERS TO TRUST IN PROVIDENCE.
IF I AM KILLED, I CAN DIE BUT ONCE, BUT TO LIVE IN CONSTANT DREAD OF IT IS TO DIE OVER AND OVER AGAIN.
(AFTER ALL, HE HAS OBSERVED, IF SOMEONE IS DETERMINED TO DO HIM HARM, AND CARES NOT ABOUT GIVING UP HIS OWN LIFE, THERE IS LITTLE THAT CAN BE DONE.)
FONDLY DO WE HOPE — FERVENTLY DO WE PRAY — THAT THIS MIGHTY SCOURGE OF WAR MAY SPEEDILY PASS AWAY.

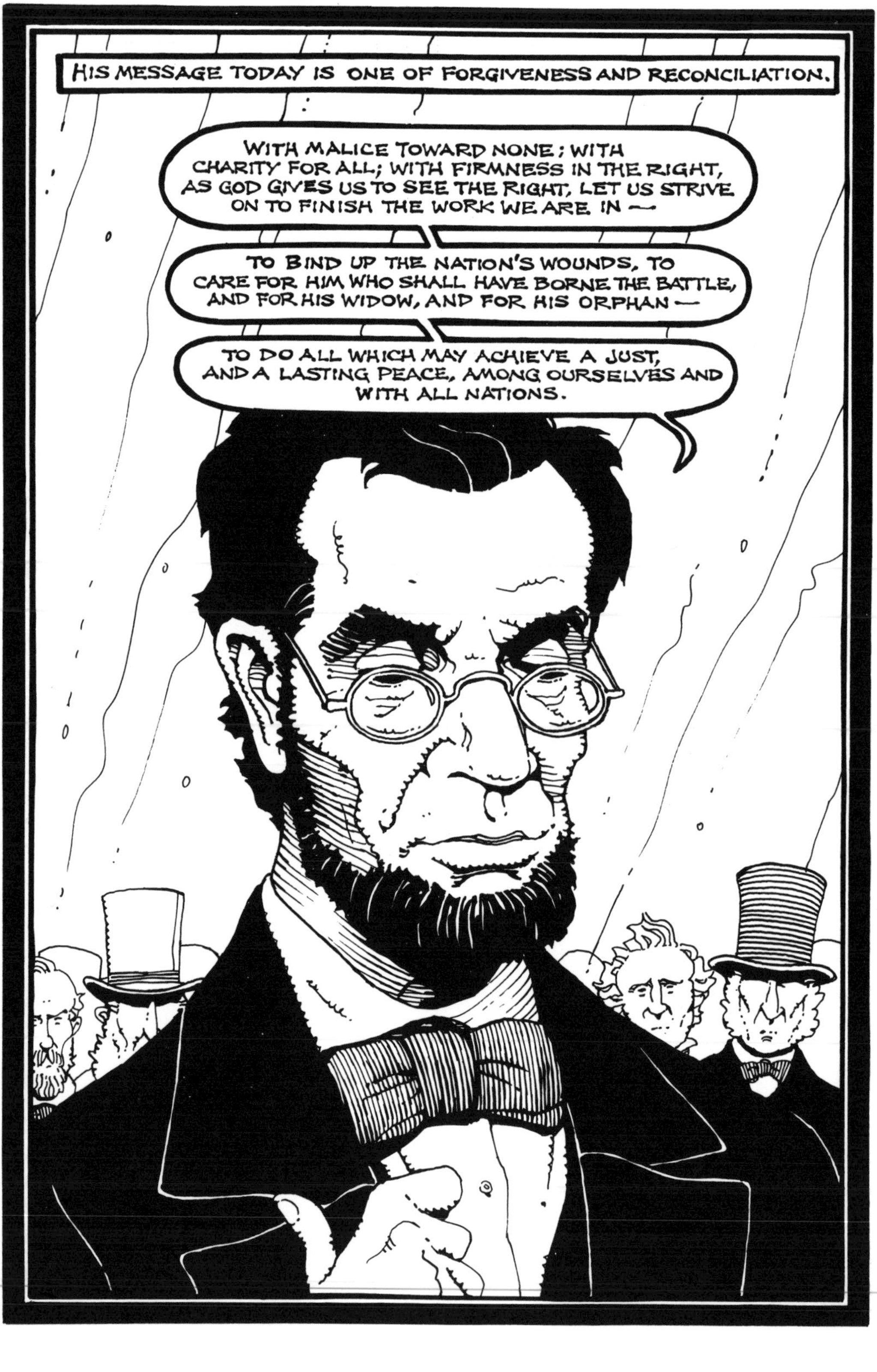
HIS MESSAGE TODAY IS ONE OF FORGIVENESS AND RECONCILIATION.
WITH MALICE TOWARD NONE; WITH CHARITY FOR ALL; WITH FIRMNESS IN THE RIGHT, AS GOD GIVES US TO SEE THE RIGHT, LET US STRIVE ON TO FINISH THE WORK WE ARE IN —
TO BIND UP THE NATION'S WOUNDS, TO CARE FOR HIM WHO SHALL HAVE BORNE THE BATTLE, AND FOR HIS WIDOW, AND FOR HIS ORPHAN —
TO DO ALL WHICH MAY ACHIEVE A JUST, AND A LASTING PEACE, AMONG OURSELVES AND WITH ALL NATIONS.

PART II.

THE CONSPIRATORS

SURRATT'S BOARDING HOUSE

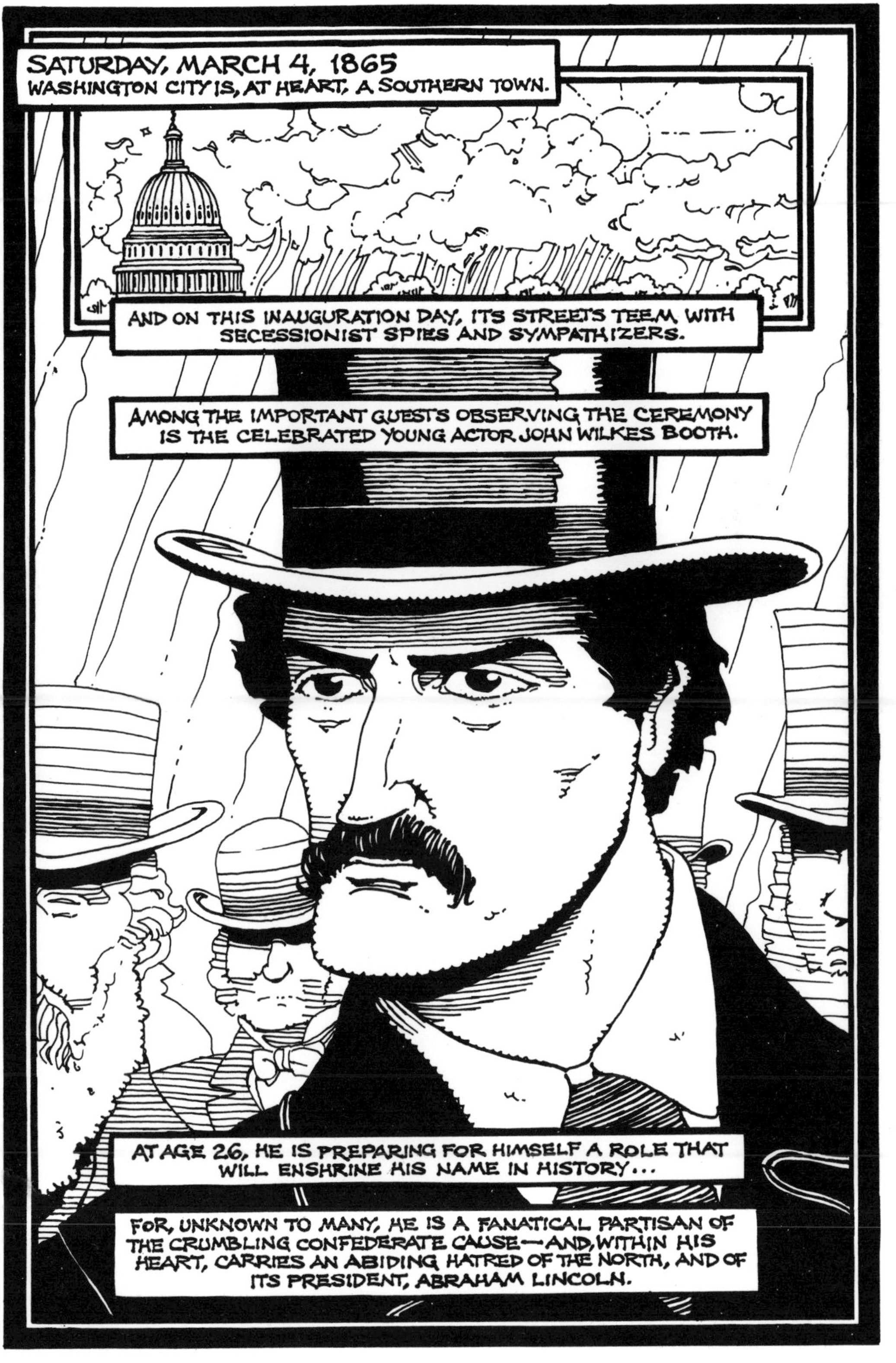
SATURDAY, MARCH 4, 1865
WASHINGTON CITY IS, AT HEART, A SOUTHERN TOWN.
AND ON THIS INAUGURATION DAY, ITS STREETS TEEM WITH SECESSIONIST SPIES AND SYMPATHIZERS.
AMONG THE IMPORTANT GUESTS OBSERVING THE CEREMONY IS THE CELEBRATED YOUNG ACTOR JOHN WILKES BOOTH.
AT AGE 26, HE IS PREPARING FOR HIMSELF A ROLE THAT WILL ENSHRINE HIS NAME IN HISTORY...
FOR, UNKNOWN TO MANY, HE IS A FANATICAL PARTISAN OF THE CRUMBLING CONFEDERATE CAUSE—AND, WITHIN HIS HEART, CARRIES AN ABIDING HATRED OF THE NORTH, AND OF ITS PRESIDENT, ABRAHAM LINCOLN.

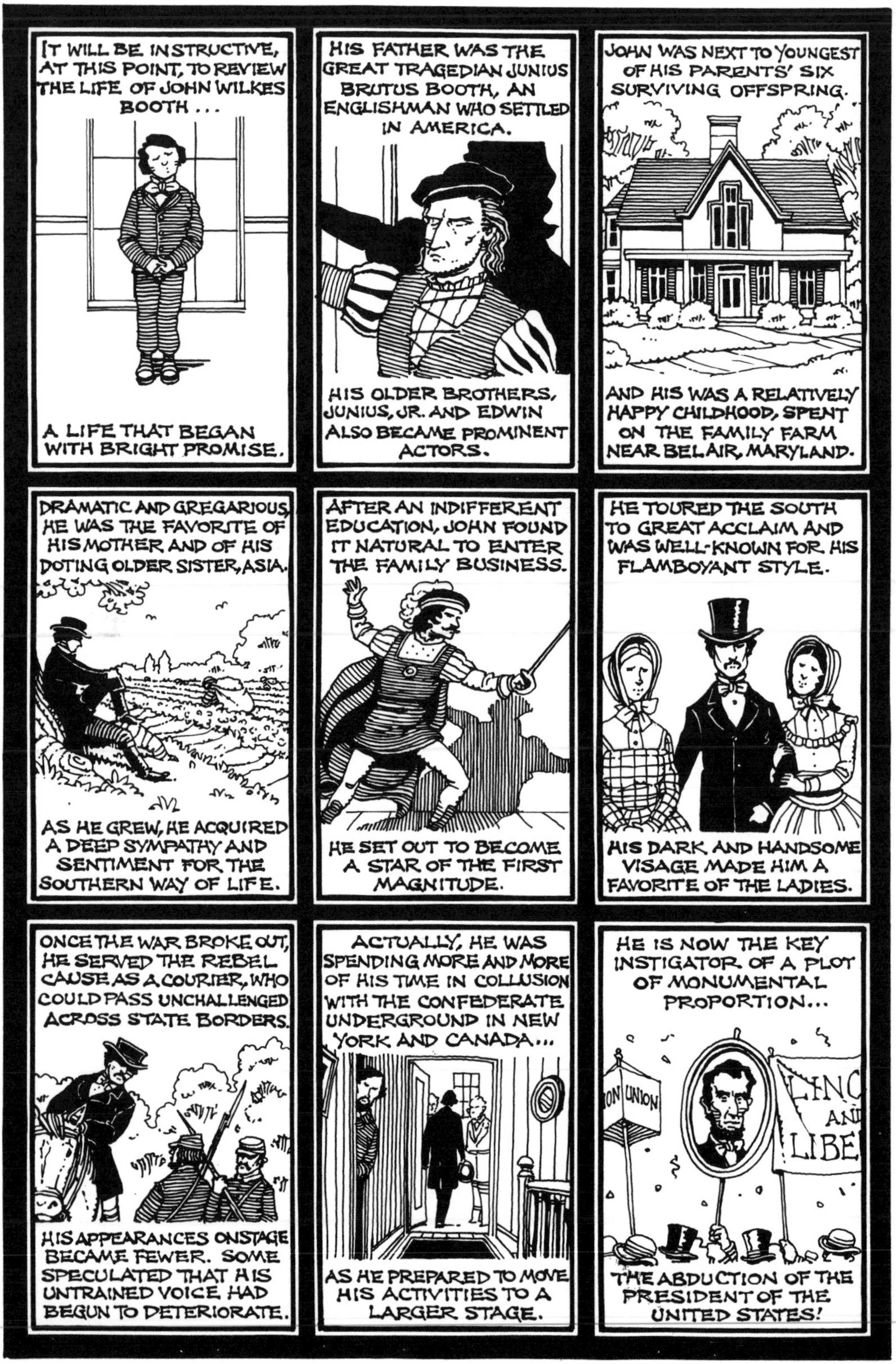
IT WILL BE INSTRUCTIVE, AT THIS POINT, TO REVIEW THE LIFE OF JOHN WILKES BOOTH ...
A LIFE THAT BEGAN WITH BRIGHT PROMISE.
HIS FATHER WAS THE GREAT TRAGEDIAN JUNIUS BRUTUS BOOTH, AN ENGLISHMAN WHO SETTLED IN AMERICA.
HIS OLDER BROTHERS, JUNIUS, JR. AND EDWIN ALSO BECAME PROMINENT ACTORS.
JOHN WAS NEXT TO YOUNGEST OF HIS PARENTS' SIX SURVIVING OFFSPRING.
AND HIS WAS A RELATIVELY HAPPY CHILDHOOD, SPENT ON THE FAMILY FARM NEAR BELAIR, MARYLAND.
DRAMATIC AND GREGARIOUS, HE WAS THE FAVORITE OF HIS MOTHER AND OF HIS DOTING OLDER SISTER, ASIA.
AS HE GREW, HE ACQUIRED A DEEP SYMPATHY AND SENTIMENT FOR THE SOUTHERN WAY OF LIFE.
AFTER AN INDIFFERENT EDUCATION, JOHN FOUND IT NATURAL TO ENTER THE FAMILY BUSINESS.
HE SET OUT TO BECOME A STAR OF THE FIRST MAGNITUDE.
HE TOURED THE SOUTH TO GREAT ACCLAIM AND WAS WELL-KNOWN FOR HIS FLAMBOYANT STYLE.
HIS DARK AND HANDSOME VISAGE MADE HIM A FAVORITE OF THE LADIES.
ONCE THE WAR BROKE OUT, HE SERVED THE REBEL CAUSE AS A COURIER, WHO COULD PASS UNCHALLENGED ACROSS STATE BORDERS.
HIS APPEARANCES ONSTAGE BECAME FEWER. SOME SPECULATED THAT HIS UNTRAINED VOICE HAD BEGUN TO DETERIORATE.
ACTUALLY, HE WAS SPENDING MORE AND MORE OF HIS TIME IN COLLUSION WITH THE CONFEDERATE UNDERGROUND IN NEW YORK AND CANADA...
AS HE PREPARED TO MOVE HIS ACTIVITIES TO A LARGER STAGE.
HE IS NOW THE KEY INSTIGATOR OF A PLOT OF MONUMENTAL PROPORTION...
UNION
THE ABDUCTION OF THE PRESIDENT OF THE UNITED STATES!

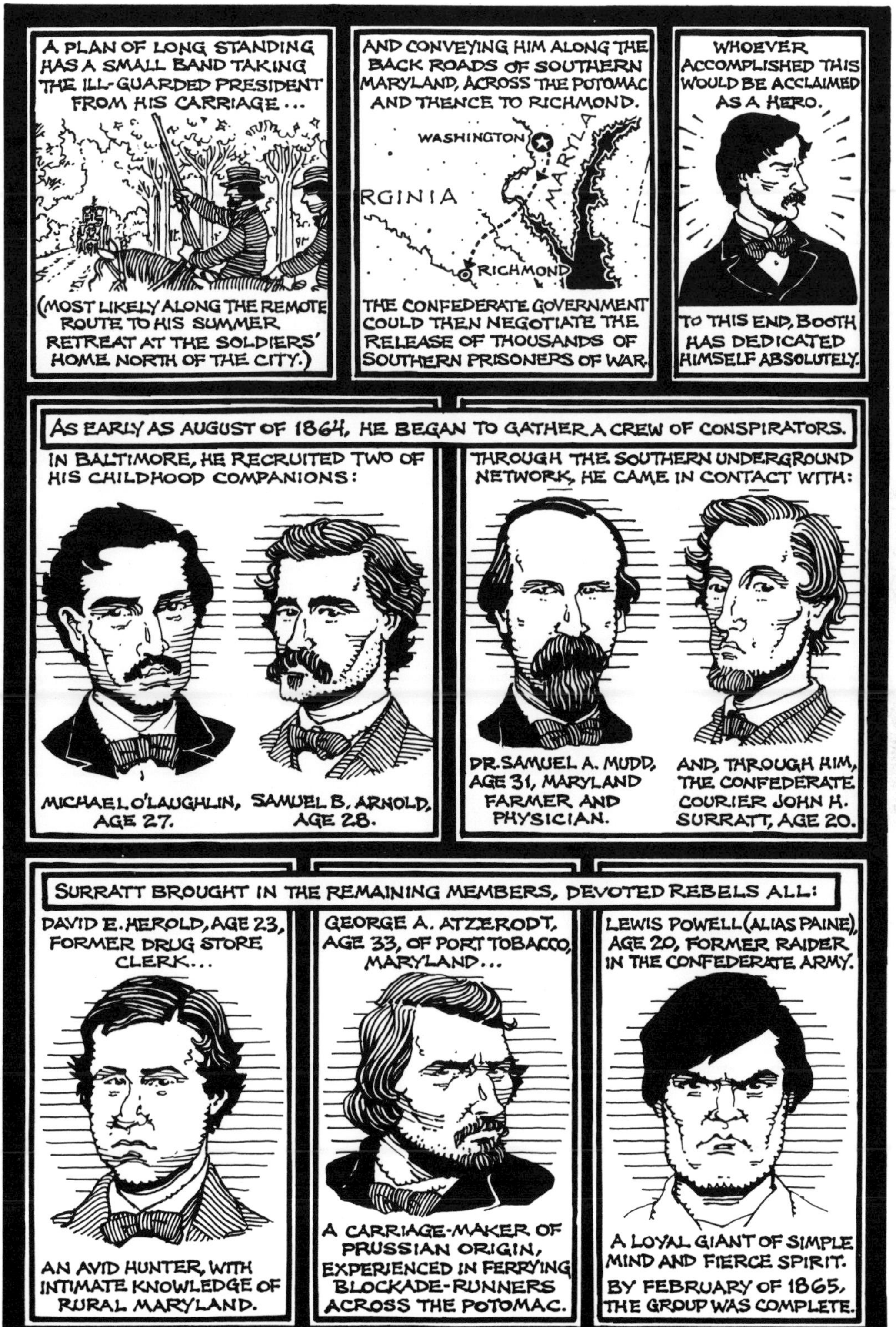

A PLAN OF LONG STANDING HAS A SMALL BAND TAKING THE ILL-GUARDED PRESIDENT FROM HIS CARRIAGE...
(MOST LIKELY ALONG THE REMOTE ROUTE TO HIS SUMMER RETREAT AT THE SOLDIERS' HOME NORTH OF THE CITY.)
AND CONVEYING HIM ALONG THE BACK ROADS OF SOUTHERN MARYLAND, ACROSS THE POTOMAC AND THENCE TO RICHMOND.
WASHINGTON
RGINIA
MARYLA
RICHMOND
THE CONFEDERATE GOVERNMENT COULD THEN NEGOTIATE THE RELEASE OF THOUSANDS OF SOUTHERN PRISONERS OF WAR.
WHOEVER ACCOMPLISHED THIS WOULD BE ACCLAIMED AS A HERO.
TO THIS END, BOOTH HAS DEDICATED HIMSELF ABSOLUTELY.
AS EARLY AS AUGUST OF 1864, HE BEGAN TO GATHER A CREW OF CONSPIRATORS.
IN BALTIMORE, HE RECRUITED TWO OF HIS CHILDHOOD COMPANIONS:
MICHAEL O'LAUGHLIN, AGE 27.
SAMUEL B. ARNOLD, AGE 28.
THROUGH THE SOUTHERN UNDERGROUND NETWORK, HE CAME IN CONTACT WITH:
DR. SAMUEL A. MUDD, AGE 31, MARYLAND FARMER AND PHYSICIAN.
AND, THROUGH HIM, THE CONFEDERATE COURIER JOHN H. SURRATT, AGE 20.
SURRATT BROUGHT IN THE REMAINING MEMBERS, DEVOTED REBELS ALL:
DAVID E. HEROLD, AGE 23, FORMER DRUG STORE CLERK...
AN AVID HUNTER, WITH INTIMATE KNOWLEDGE OF RURAL MARYLAND.
GEORGE A. ATZERODT, AGE 33, OF PORT TOBACCO, MARYLAND...
A CARRIAGE-MAKER OF PRUSSIAN ORIGIN, EXPERIENCED IN FERRYING BLOCKADE-RUNNERS ACROSS THE POTOMAC.
LEWIS POWELL (ALIAS PAINE), AGE 20, FORMER RAIDER IN THE CONFEDERATE ARMY.
A LOYAL GIANT OF SIMPLE MIND AND FIERCE SPIRIT.
BY FEBRUARY OF 1865, THE GROUP WAS COMPLETE.

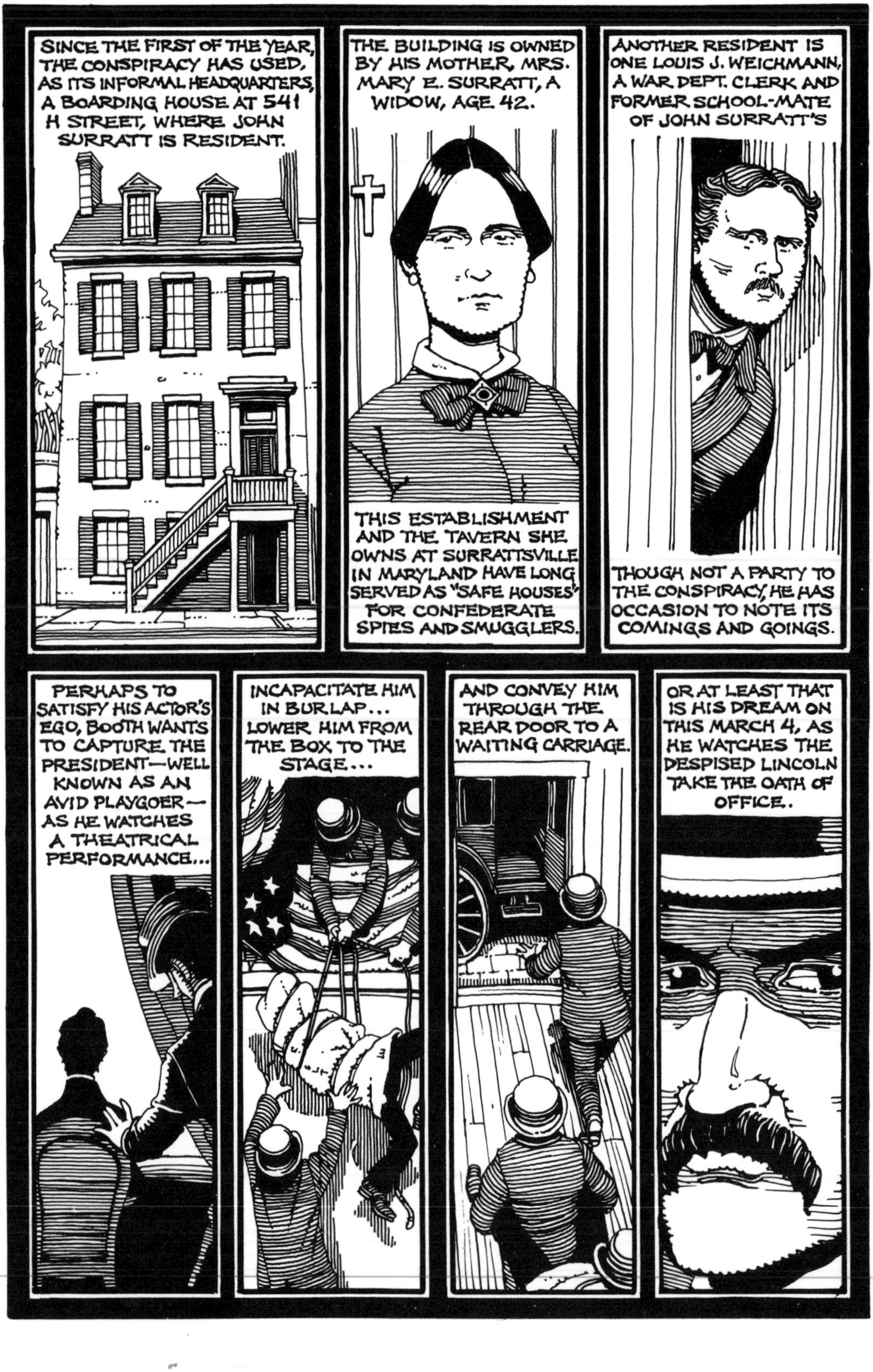
SINCE THE FIRST OF THE YEAR, THE CONSPIRACY HAS USED, AS ITS INFORMAL HEADQUARTERS, A BOARDING HOUSE AT 541 H STREET, WHERE JOHN SURRATT IS RESIDENT.
THE BUILDING IS OWNED BY HIS MOTHER, MRS. MARY E. SURRATT, A WIDOW, AGE 42.
THIS ESTABLISHMENT AND THE TAVERN SHE OWNS AT SURRATTSVILLE IN MARYLAND HAVE LONG SERVED AS "SAFE HOUSES" FOR CONFEDERATE SPIES AND SMUGGLERS.
ANOTHER RESIDENT IS ONE LOUIS J. WEICHMANN, A WAR DEPT. CLERK AND FORMER SCHOOL-MATE OF JOHN SURRATT'S
THOUGH NOT A PARTY TO THE CONSPIRACY, HE HAS OCCASION TO NOTE ITS COMINGS AND GOINGS.
PERHAPS TO SATISFY HIS ACTOR'S EGO, BOOTH WANTS TO CAPTURE THE PRESIDENT—WELL KNOWN AS AN AVID PLAYGOER—AS HE WATCHES A THEATRICAL PERFORMANCE...
INCAPACITATE HIM IN BURLAP... LOWER HIM FROM THE BOX TO THE STAGE...
AND CONVEY HIM THROUGH THE REAR DOOR TO A WAITING CARRIAGE.
OR AT LEAST THAT IS HIS DREAM ON THIS MARCH 4, AS HE WATCHES THE DESPISED LINCOLN TAKE THE OATH OF OFFICE.

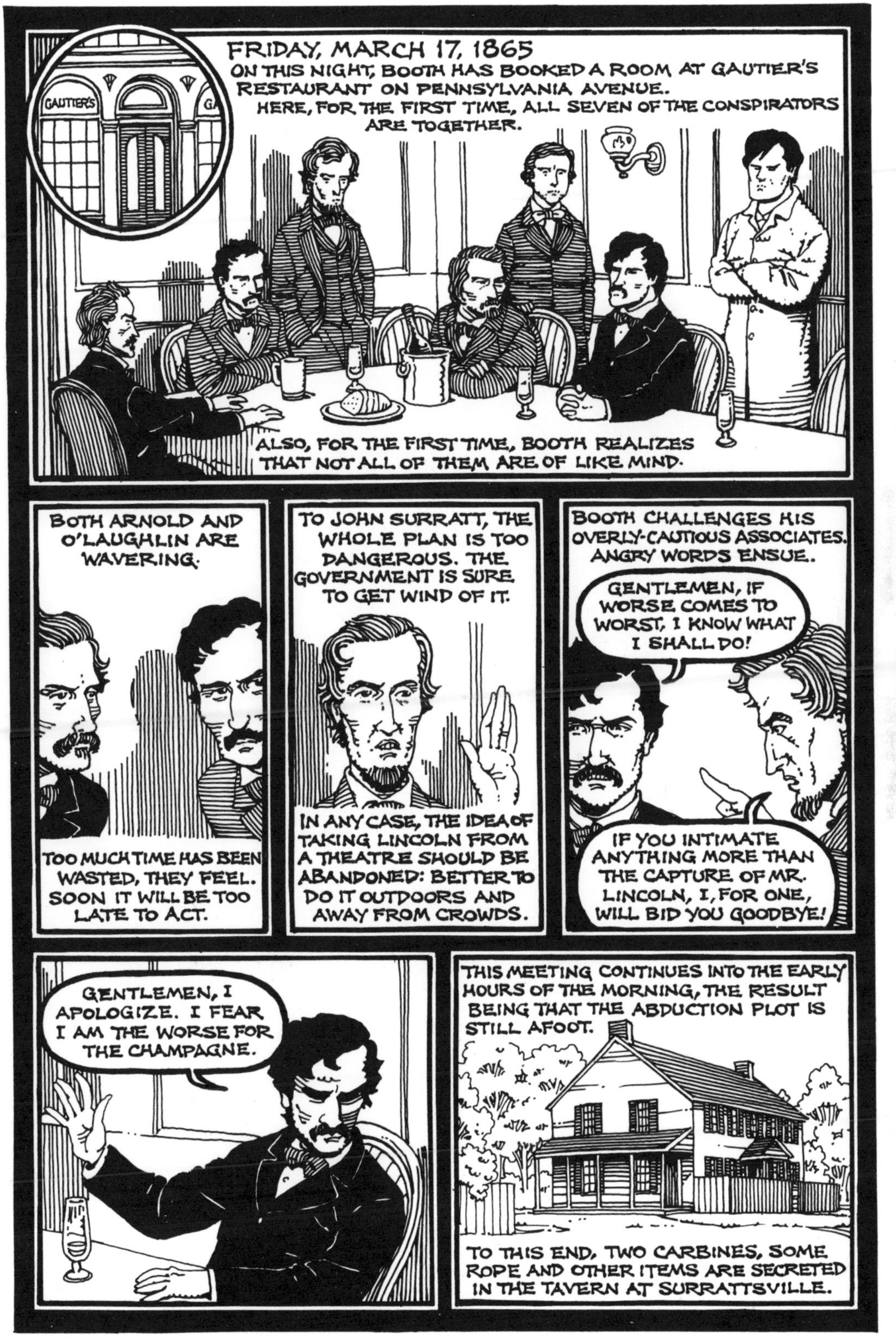
FRIDAY, MARCH 17, 1865
ON THIS NIGHT, BOOTH HAS BOOKED A ROOM AT GAUTIER'S RESTAURANT ON PENNSYLVANIA AVENUE.
HERE, FOR THE FIRST TIME, ALL SEVEN OF THE CONSPIRATORS ARE TOGETHER.
GAUTIER'S
ALSO, FOR THE FIRST TIME, BOOTH REALIZES THAT NOT ALL OF THEM ARE OF LIKE MIND.
BOTH ARNOLD AND O'LAUGHLIN ARE WAVERING.
TOO MUCH TIME HAS BEEN WASTED, THEY FEEL. SOON IT WILL BE TOO LATE TO ACT.
TO JOHN SURRATT, THE WHOLE PLAN IS TOO DANGEROUS. THE GOVERNMENT IS SURE TO GET WIND OF IT.
IN ANY CASE, THE IDEA OF TAKING LINCOLN FROM A THEATRE SHOULD BE ABANDONED: BETTER TO DO IT OUTDOORS AND AWAY FROM CROWDS.
BOOTH CHALLENGES HIS OVERLY-CAUTIOUS ASSOCIATES. ANGRY WORDS ENSUE.
GENTLEMEN, IF WORSE COMES TO WORST, I KNOW WHAT I SHALL DO!
IF YOU INTIMATE ANYTHING MORE THAN THE CAPTURE OF MR. LINCOLN, I, FOR ONE, WILL BID YOU GOODBYE!
GENTLEMEN, I APOLOGIZE. I FEAR I AM THE WORSE FOR THE CHAMPAGNE.
THIS MEETING CONTINUES INTO THE EARLY HOURS OF THE MORNING, THE RESULT BEING THAT THE ABDUCTION PLOT IS STILL AFOOT.
TO THIS END, TWO CARBINES, SOME ROPE AND OTHER ITEMS ARE SECRETED IN THE TAVERN AT SURRATTSVILLE.

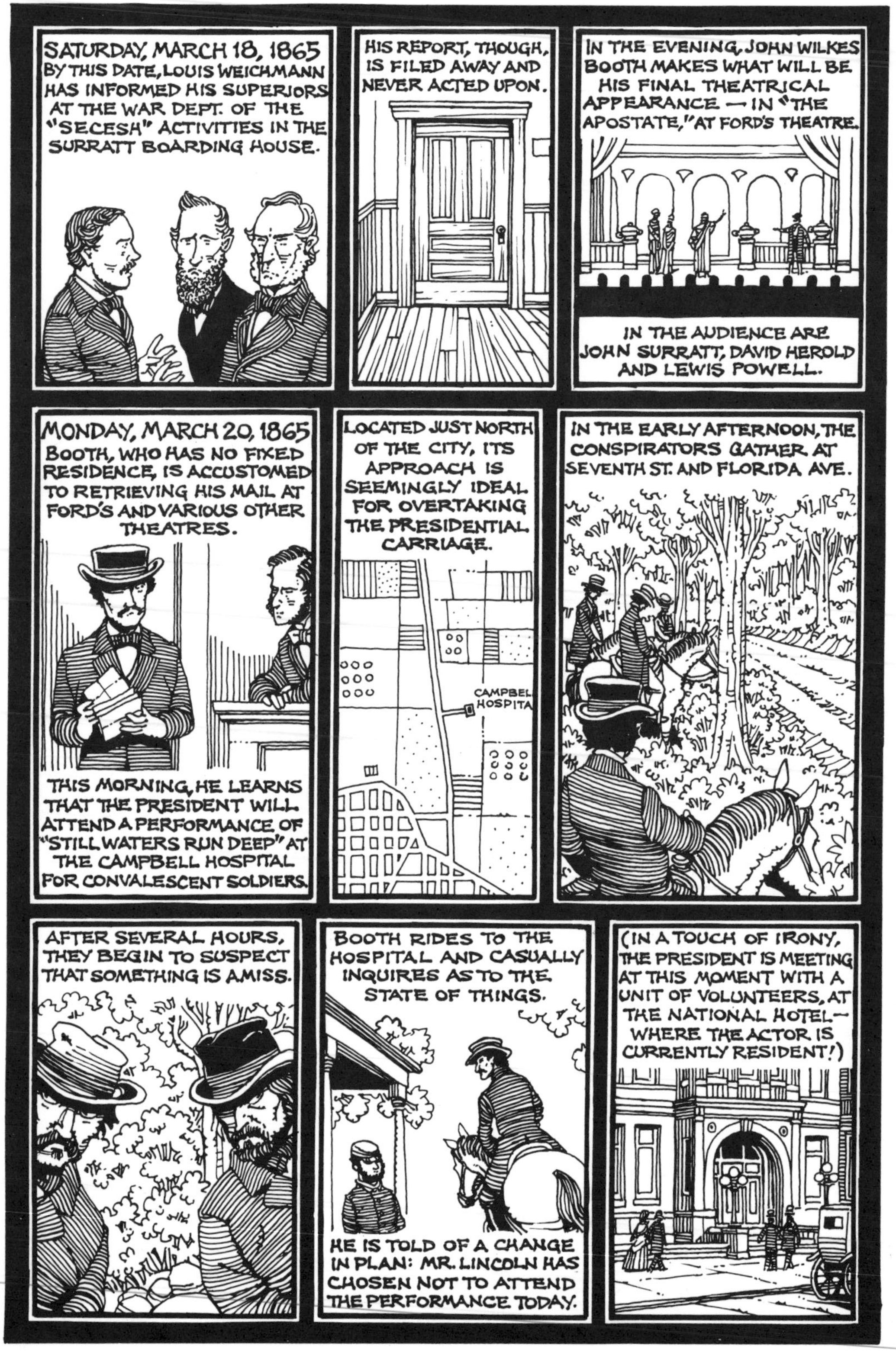

SATURDAY, MARCH 18, 1865
BY THIS DATE, LOUIS WEICHMANN HAS INFORMED HIS SUPERIORS AT THE WAR DEPT. OF THE "SECESH" ACTIVITIES IN THE SURRATT BOARDING HOUSE.
HIS REPORT, THOUGH, IS FILED AWAY AND NEVER ACTED UPON.
IN THE EVENING, JOHN WILKES BOOTH MAKES WHAT WILL BE HIS FINAL THEATRICAL APPEARANCE — IN "THE APOSTATE," AT FORD'S THEATRE.
IN THE AUDIENCE ARE JOHN SURRATT, DAVID HEROLD AND LEWIS POWELL.
MONDAY, MARCH 20, 1865
BOOTH, WHO HAS NO FIXED RESIDENCE, IS ACCUSTOMED TO RETRIEVING HIS MAIL AT FORD'S AND VARIOUS OTHER THEATRES.
THIS MORNING, HE LEARNS THAT THE PRESIDENT WILL ATTEND A PERFORMANCE OF "STILL WATERS RUN DEEP" AT THE CAMPBELL HOSPITAL FOR CONVALESCENT SOLDIERS.
LOCATED JUST NORTH OF THE CITY, ITS APPROACH IS SEEMINGLY IDEAL FOR OVERTAKING THE PRESIDENTIAL CARRIAGE.
CAMPBEL
HOSPITA
IN THE EARLY AFTERNOON, THE CONSPIRATORS GATHER AT SEVENTH ST. AND FLORIDA AVE.
AFTER SEVERAL HOURS, THEY BEGIN TO SUSPECT THAT SOMETHING IS AMISS.
BOOTH RIDES TO THE HOSPITAL AND CASUALLY INQUIRES AS TO THE STATE OF THINGS.
HE IS TOLD OF A CHANGE IN PLAN: MR. LINCOLN HAS CHOSEN NOT TO ATTEND THE PERFORMANCE TODAY.
(IN A TOUCH OF IRONY, THE PRESIDENT IS MEETING AT THIS MOMENT WITH A UNIT OF VOLUNTEERS, AT THE NATIONAL HOTEL— WHERE THE ACTOR IS CURRENTLY RESIDENT!)

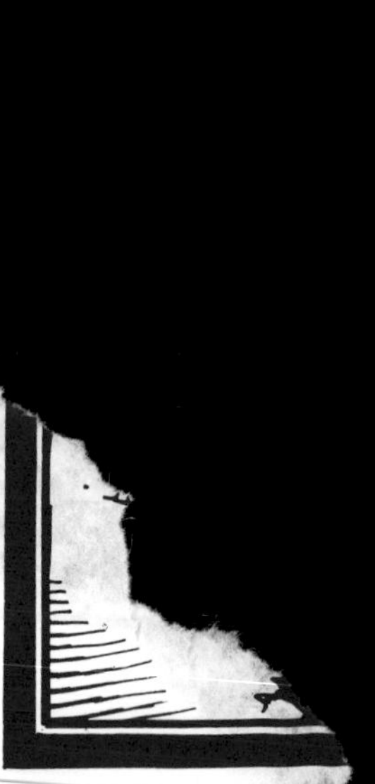

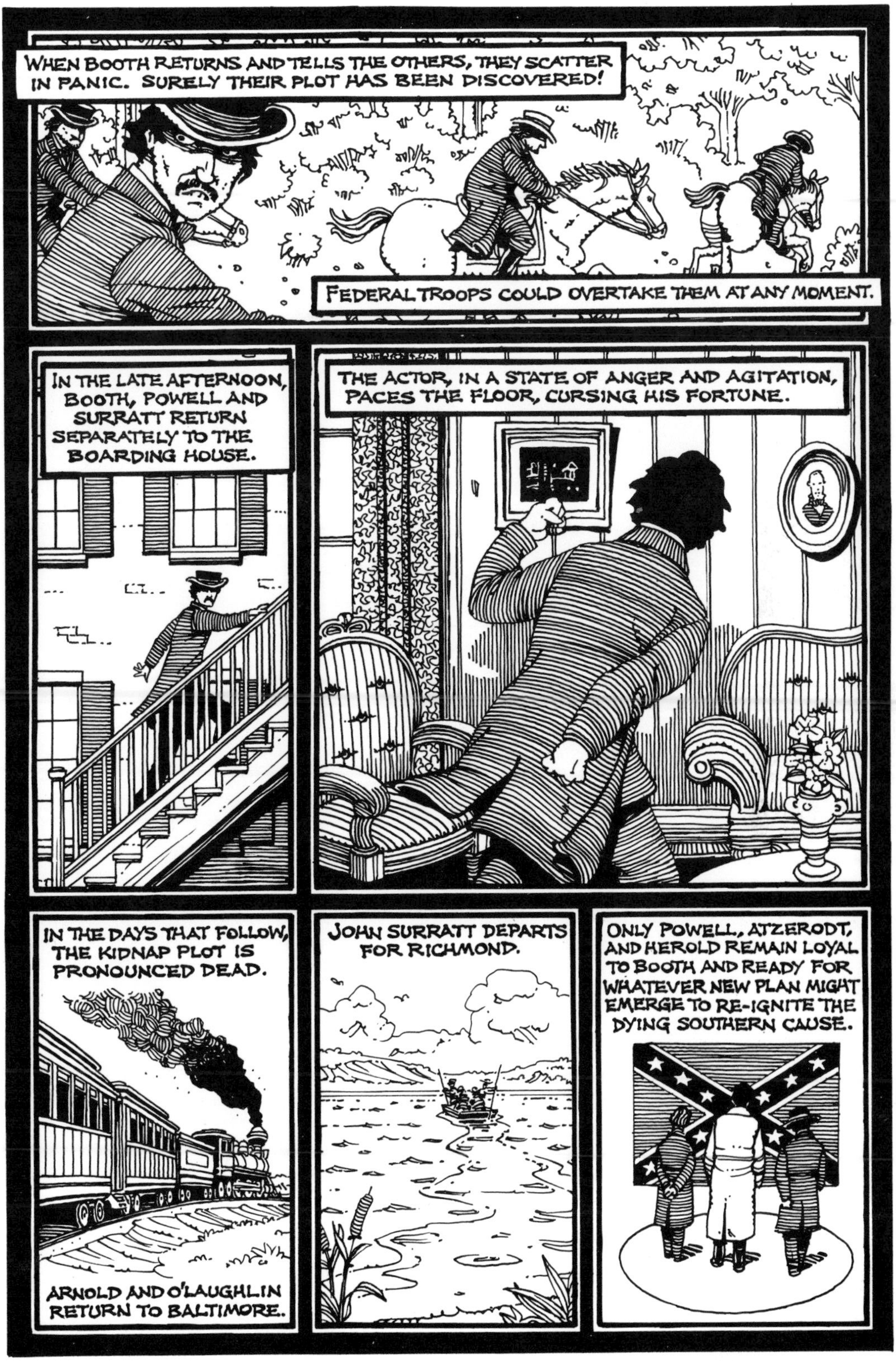
WHEN BOOTH RETURNS AND TELLS THE OTHERS, THEY SCATTER IN PANIC. SURELY THEIR PLOT HAS BEEN DISCOVERED!
FEDERAL TROOPS COULD OVERTAKE THEM AT ANY MOMENT.
IN THE LATE AFTERNOON, BOOTH, POWELL AND SURRATT RETURN SEPARATELY TO THE BOARDING HOUSE.
THE ACTOR, IN A STATE OF ANGER AND AGITATION, PACES THE FLOOR, CURSING HIS FORTUNE.
IN THE DAYS THAT FOLLOW, THE KIDNAP PLOT IS PRONOUNCED DEAD.
ARNOLD AND O'LAUGHLIN RETURN TO BALTIMORE.
JOHN SURRATT DEPARTS FOR RICHMOND.
ONLY POWELL, ATZERODT, AND HEROLD REMAIN LOYAL TO BOOTH AND READY FOR WHATEVER NEW PLAN MIGHT EMERGE TO RE-IGNITE THE DYING SOUTHERN CAUSE.

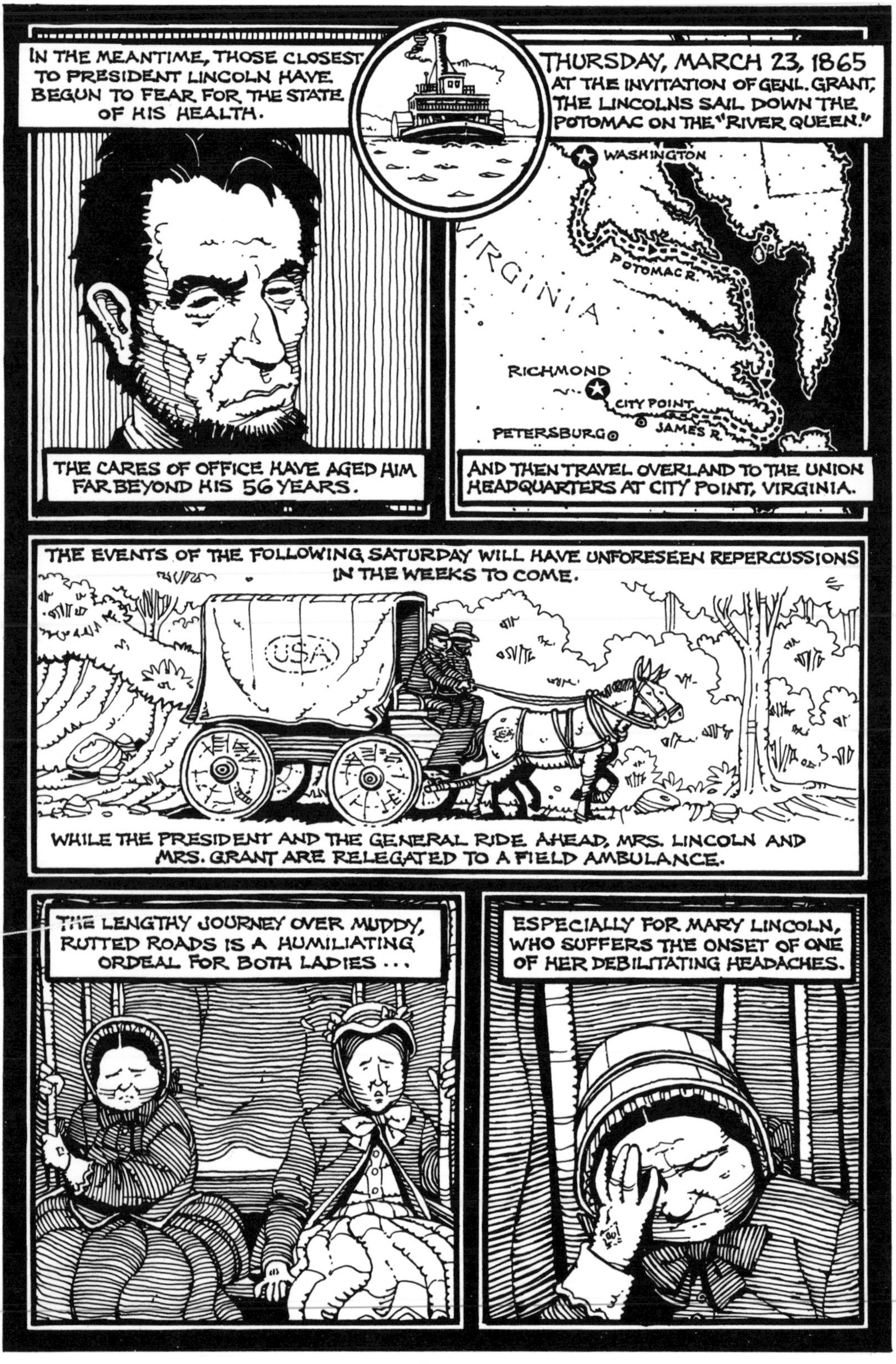
IN THE MEANTIME, THOSE CLOSEST TO PRESIDENT LINCOLN HAVE BEGUN TO FEAR FOR THE STATE OF HIS HEALTH.
THURSDAY, MARCH 23, 1865
AT THE INVITATION OF GENL. GRANT, THE LINCOLNS SAIL DOWN THE POTOMAC ON THE "RIVER QUEEN."
WASHINGTON
VIRGINIA
POTOMAC R.
RICHMOND
CITY POINT
JAMES R.
PETERSBURG
THE CARES OF OFFICE HAVE AGED HIM FAR BEYOND HIS 56 YEARS.
AND THEN TRAVEL OVERLAND TO THE UNION HEADQUARTERS AT CITY POINT, VIRGINIA.
THE EVENTS OF THE FOLLOWING SATURDAY WILL HAVE UNFORESEEN REPERCUSSIONS IN THE WEEKS TO COME.
USA
WHILE THE PRESIDENT AND THE GENERAL RIDE AHEAD, MRS. LINCOLN AND MRS. GRANT ARE RELEGATED TO A FIELD AMBULANCE.
THE LENGTHY JOURNEY OVER MUDDY, RUTTED ROADS IS A HUMILIATING ORDEAL FOR BOTH LADIES . . .
ESPECIALLY FOR MARY LINCOLN, WHO SUFFERS THE ONSET OF ONE OF HER DEBILITATING HEADACHES.

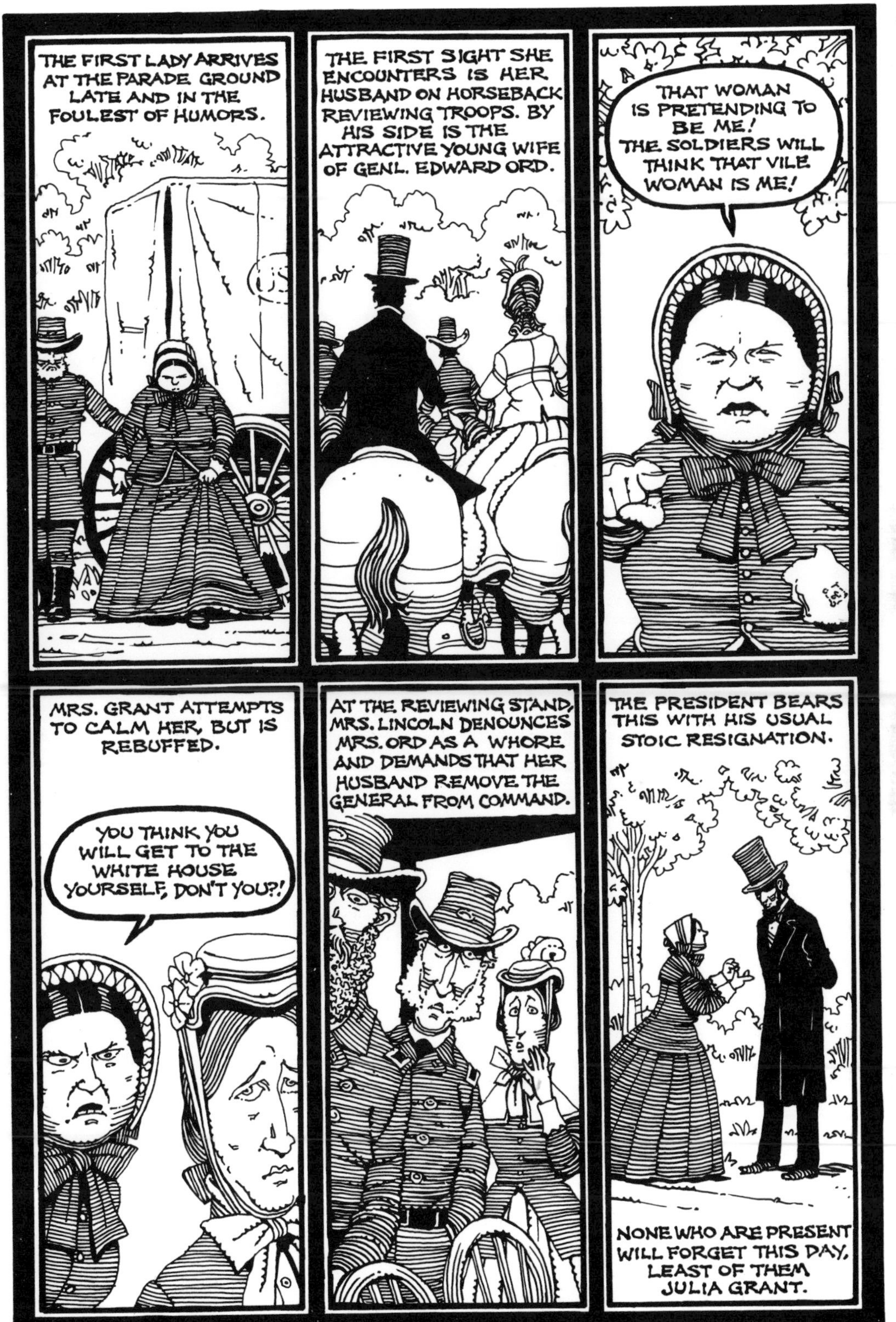
THE FIRST LADY ARRIVES AT THE PARADE GROUND LATE AND IN THE FOULEST OF HUMORS.
US
THE FIRST SIGHT SHE ENCOUNTERS IS HER HUSBAND ON HORSEBACK REVIEWING TROOPS. BY HIS SIDE IS THE ATTRACTIVE YOUNG WIFE OF GENL. EDWARD ORD.
THAT WOMAN IS PRETENDING TO BE ME! THE SOLDIERS WILL THINK THAT VILE WOMAN IS ME!
MRS. GRANT ATTEMPTS TO CALM HER, BUT IS REBUFFED.
YOU THINK YOU WILL GET TO THE WHITE HOUSE YOURSELF, DON'T YOU?!
AT THE REVIEWING STAND, MRS. LINCOLN DENOUNCES MRS. ORD AS A WHORE AND DEMANDS THAT HER HUSBAND REMOVE THE GENERAL FROM COMMAND.
THE PRESIDENT BEARS THIS WITH HIS USUAL STOIC RESIGNATION.
NONE WHO ARE PRESENT WILL FORGET THIS DAY, LEAST OF THEM JULIA GRANT.

BY NOW IT IS PLAIN TO MOST AMERICANS THAT THE SOUTHERN CAUSE IS DOOMED.

NOT, HOWEVER, TO JOHN WILKES BOOTH, WHO SPENDS SEVERAL DAYS IN NEW YORK AND BOSTON MEETING WITH CONFEDERATE OPERATIVES.

MONDAY, APRIL 3, 1865
THE SOUTHERN CAPITAL OF RICHMOND FALLS TO THE UNION ARMY.

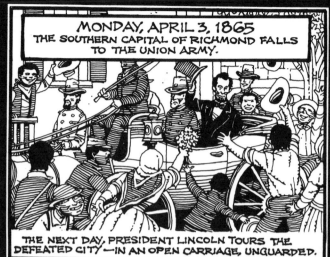

THE NEXT DAY, PRESIDENT LINCOLN TOURS THE DEFEATED CITY — IN AN OPEN CARRIAGE, UNGUARDED.

SUNDAY, APRIL 9, 1865
GENL. LEE SURRENDERS TO GENL. GRANT AT APPOMATTOX COURT HOUSE, VIRGINIA. PRESENT AT THE CEREMONY IS ROBERT TODD LINCOLN, AGE 21, THE PRESIDENT'S ELDEST SON.

FROM THIS MOMENT, THE WAR IS EFFECTIVELY OVER.

THE CITY OF WASHINGTON STAGES A GRAND CELEBRATION THAT WILL LAST SEVERAL DAYS.

LINCOLN RETURNS TO GREAT ADULATION. TO THOSE CLOSE TO HIM, HE SEEMS BUOYANT, TRANSFORMED.

MONDAY, APRIL 10, 1865
ON THIS DAY, HE VISITS THE STUDIO OF ALEXANDER GARDNER FOR A SERIES OF PORTRAITS THAT REFLECT HIS MOOD.

THEY WILL TURN OUT TO BE HIS LAST IMAGES.

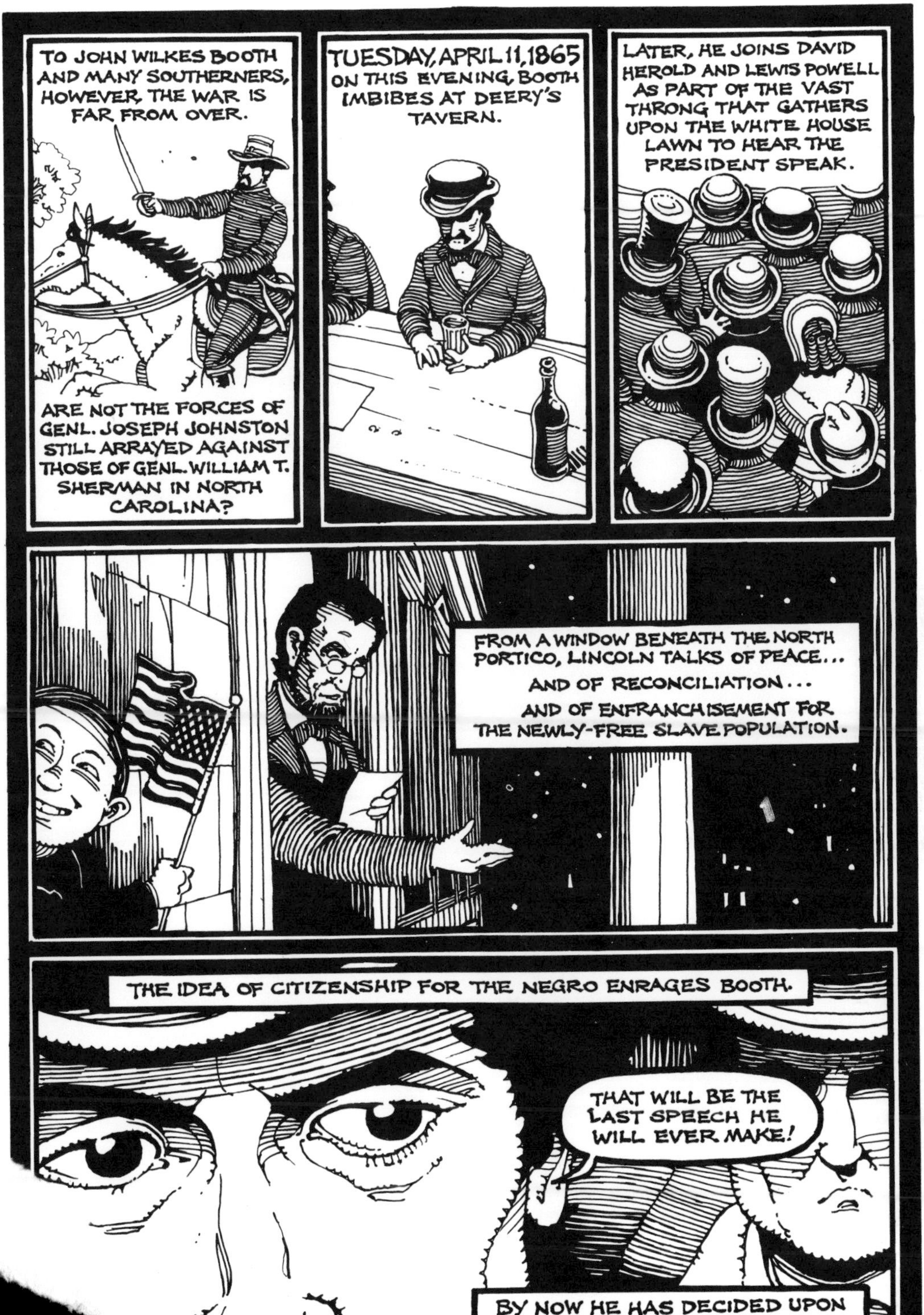
TO JOHN WILKES BOOTH AND MANY SOUTHERNERS, HOWEVER, THE WAR IS FAR FROM OVER.
ARE NOT THE FORCES OF GENL. JOSEPH JOHNSTON STILL ARRAYED AGAINST THOSE OF GENL. WILLIAM T. SHERMAN IN NORTH CAROLINA?
TUESDAY, APRIL 11, 1865
ON THIS EVENING, BOOTH IMBIBES AT DEERY'S TAVERN.
LATER, HE JOINS DAVID HEROLD AND LEWIS POWELL AS PART OF THE VAST THRONG THAT GATHERS UPON THE WHITE HOUSE LAWN TO HEAR THE PRESIDENT SPEAK.
FROM A WINDOW BENEATH THE NORTH PORTICO, LINCOLN TALKS OF PEACE...
AND OF RECONCILIATION...
AND OF ENFRANCHISEMENT FOR THE NEWLY-FREE SLAVE POPULATION.
THE IDEA OF CITIZENSHIP FOR THE NEGRO ENRAGES BOOTH.
THAT WILL BE THE LAST SPEECH HE WILL EVER MAKE!
BY NOW HE HAS DECIDED UPON HIS ULTIMATE COURSE.

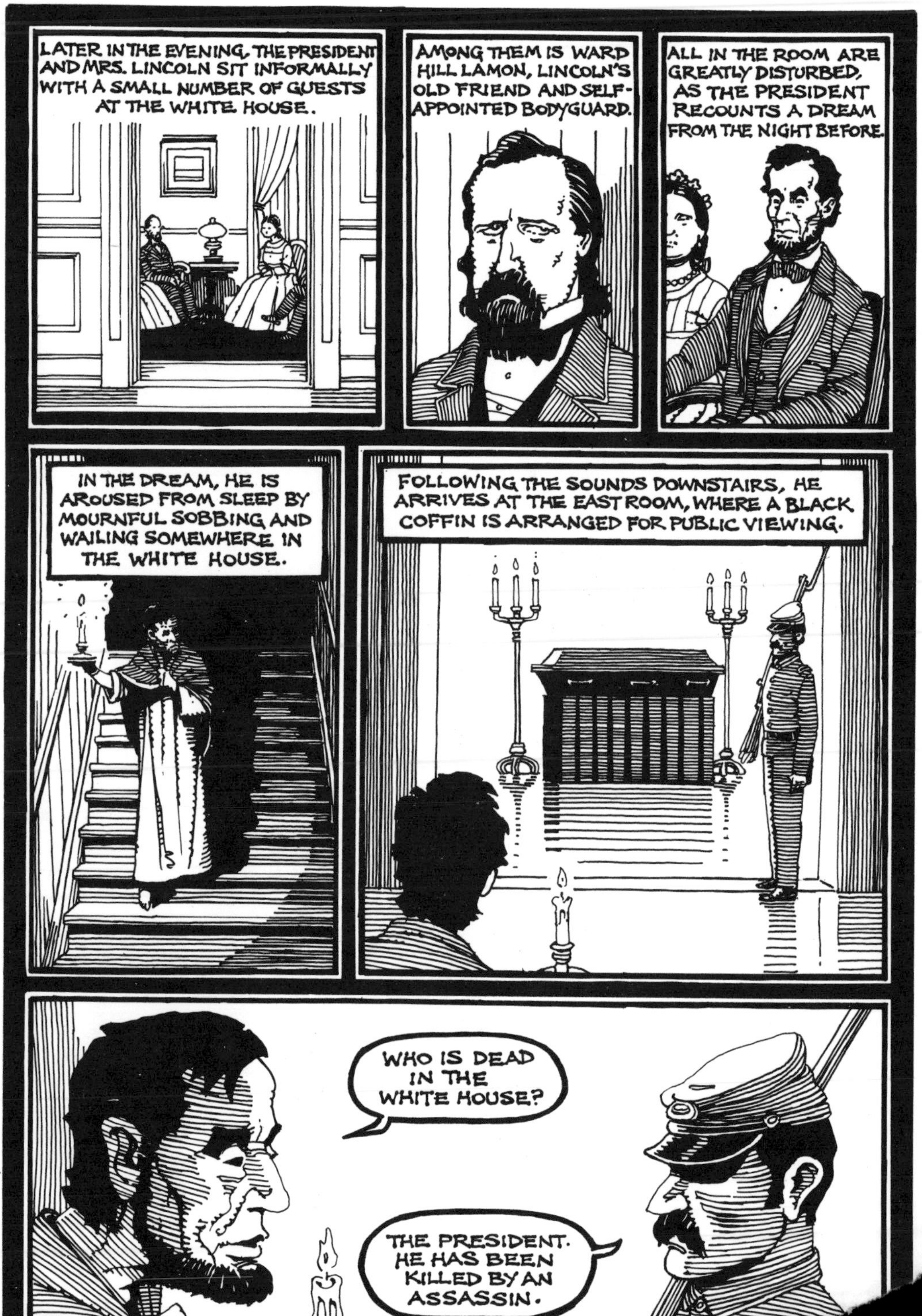
LATER IN THE EVENING, THE PRESIDENT AND MRS. LINCOLN SIT INFORMALLY WITH A SMALL NUMBER OF GUESTS AT THE WHITE HOUSE.
AMONG THEM IS WARD HILL LAMON, LINCOLN'S OLD FRIEND AND SELF-APPOINTED BODYGUARD.
ALL IN THE ROOM ARE GREATLY DISTURBED, AS THE PRESIDENT RECOUNTS A DREAM FROM THE NIGHT BEFORE.
IN THE DREAM, HE IS AROUSED FROM SLEEP BY MOURNFUL SOBBING AND WAILING SOMEWHERE IN THE WHITE HOUSE.
FOLLOWING THE SOUNDS DOWNSTAIRS, HE ARRIVES AT THE EAST ROOM, WHERE A BLACK COFFIN IS ARRANGED FOR PUBLIC VIEWING.
WHO IS DEAD IN THE WHITE HOUSE?
THE PRESIDENT. HE HAS BEEN KILLED BY AN ASSASSIN.

PART III.
GOOD FRIDAY

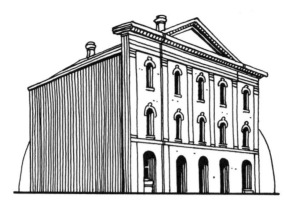

FORD'S THEATRE

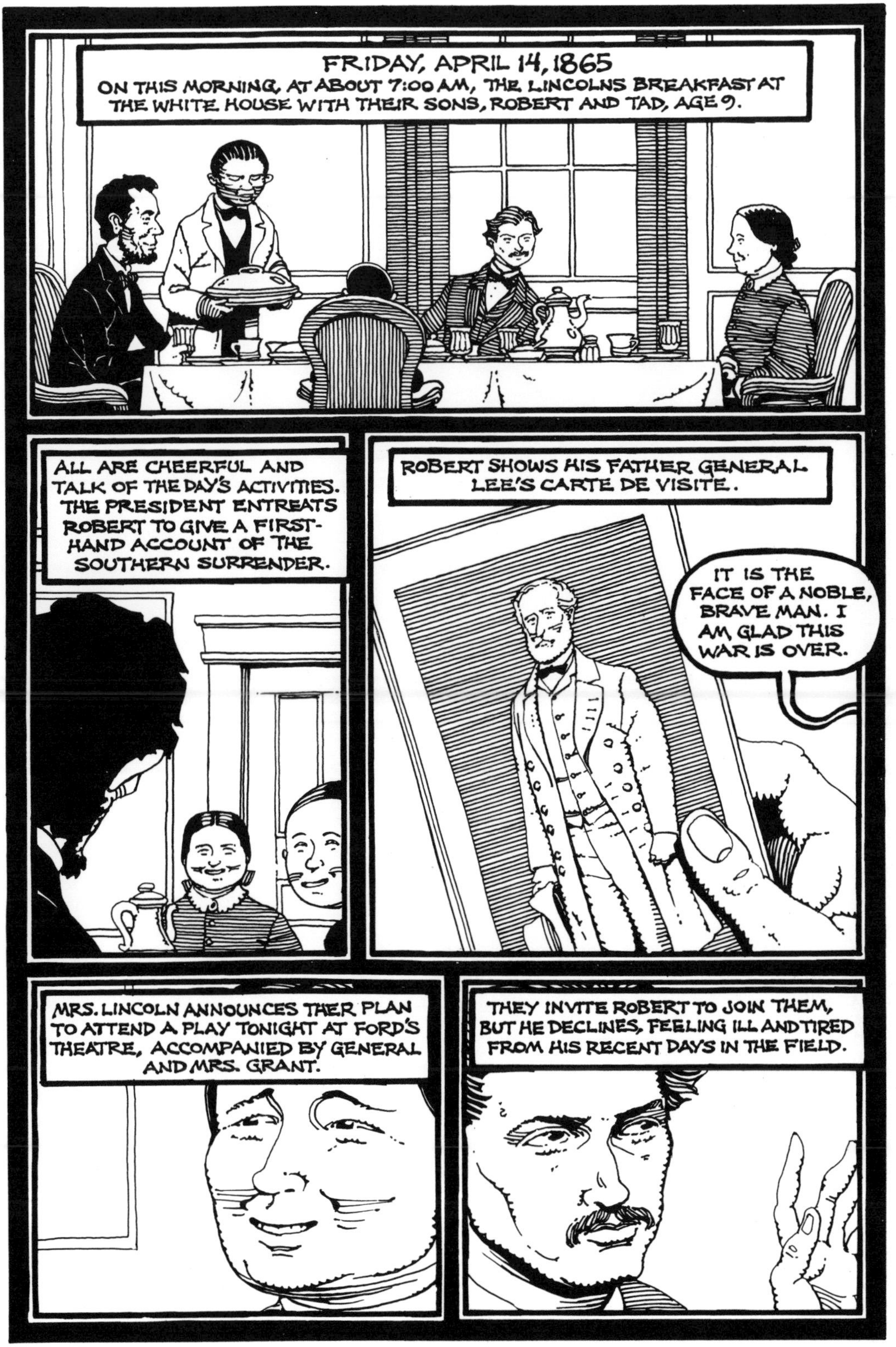

FRIDAY, APRIL 14, 1865
ON THIS MORNING, AT ABOUT 7:00 AM, THE LINCOLNS BREAKFAST AT THE WHITE HOUSE WITH THEIR SONS, ROBERT AND TAD, AGE 9.
ALL ARE CHEERFUL AND TALK OF THE DAY'S ACTIVITIES. THE PRESIDENT ENTREATS ROBERT TO GIVE A FIRST-HAND ACCOUNT OF THE SOUTHERN SURRENDER.
ROBERT SHOWS HIS FATHER GENERAL LEE'S CARTE DE VISITE.
IT IS THE FACE OF A NOBLE, BRAVE MAN. I AM GLAD THIS WAR IS OVER.
MRS. LINCOLN ANNOUNCES THER PLAN TO ATTEND A PLAY TONIGHT AT FORD'S THEATRE, ACCOMPANIED BY GENERAL AND MRS. GRANT.
THEY INVITE ROBERT TO JOIN THEM, BUT HE DECLINES, FEELING ILL AND TIRED FROM HIS RECENT DAYS IN THE FIELD.

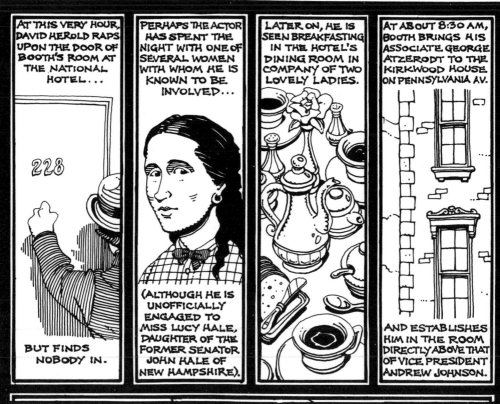

AT THIS VERY HOUR, DAVID HEROLD RAPS UPON THE DOOR OF BOOTH'S ROOM AT THE NATIONAL HOTEL...

228

BUT FINDS NOBODY IN.

PERHAPS THE ACTOR HAS SPENT THE NIGHT WITH ONE OF SEVERAL WOMEN WITH WHOM HE IS KNOWN TO BE INVOLVED...

(ALTHOUGH HE IS UNOFFICIALLY ENGAGED TO MISS LUCY HALE, DAUGHTER OF THE FORMER SENATOR JOHN HALE OF NEW HAMPSHIRE).

LATER ON, HE IS SEEN BREAKFASTING IN THE HOTEL'S DINING ROOM IN COMPANY OF TWO LOVELY LADIES.

AT ABOUT 8:30 AM, BOOTH BRINGS HIS ASSOCIATE GEORGE ATZERODT TO THE KIRKWOOD HOUSE ON PENNSYLVANIA AV.

AND ESTABLISHES HIM IN THE ROOM DIRECTLY ABOVE THAT OF VICE PRESIDENT ANDREW JOHNSON.

IN COMPANY OF HEROLD AND LEWIS POWELL, HE THEN PATRONIZES HIS FAVORITE BARBER, FOR A TRIM OF HIS HAIR AND REFURBISHMENT OF HIS FACIAL BEAUTY.

HE IS NOW READY TO BE MASTER OF HIS DAY!

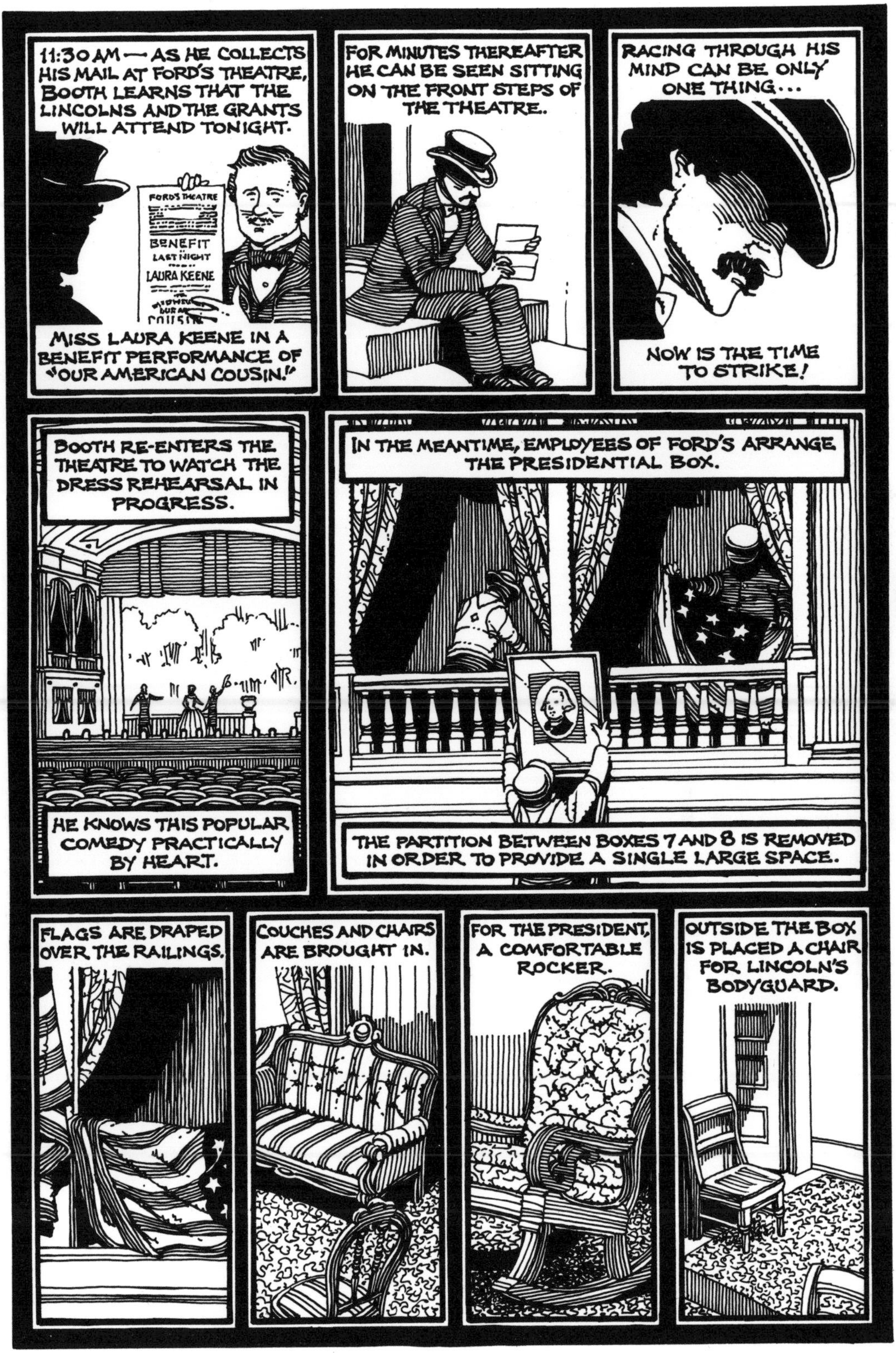
11:30 AM — AS HE COLLECTS HIS MAIL AT FORD'S THEATRE, BOOTH LEARNS THAT THE LINCOLNS AND THE GRANTS WILL ATTEND TONIGHT.
FORD'S THEATRE
BENEFIT
LAST NIGHT
LAURA KEENE
MISS LAURA KEENE IN A BENEFIT PERFORMANCE OF "OUR AMERICAN COUSIN."
FOR MINUTES THEREAFTER HE CAN BE SEEN SITTING ON THE FRONT STEPS OF THE THEATRE.
RACING THROUGH HIS MIND CAN BE ONLY ONE THING...
NOW IS THE TIME TO STRIKE!
BOOTH RE-ENTERS THE THEATRE TO WATCH THE DRESS REHEARSAL IN PROGRESS.
HE KNOWS THIS POPULAR COMEDY PRACTICALLY BY HEART.
IN THE MEANTIME, EMPLOYEES OF FORD'S ARRANGE THE PRESIDENTIAL BOX.
THE PARTITION BETWEEN BOXES 7 AND 8 IS REMOVED IN ORDER TO PROVIDE A SINGLE LARGE SPACE.
FLAGS ARE DRAPED OVER THE RAILINGS.
COUCHES AND CHAIRS ARE BROUGHT IN.
FOR THE PRESIDENT, A COMFORTABLE ROCKER.
OUTSIDE THE BOX IS PLACED A CHAIR FOR LINCOLN'S BODYGUARD.

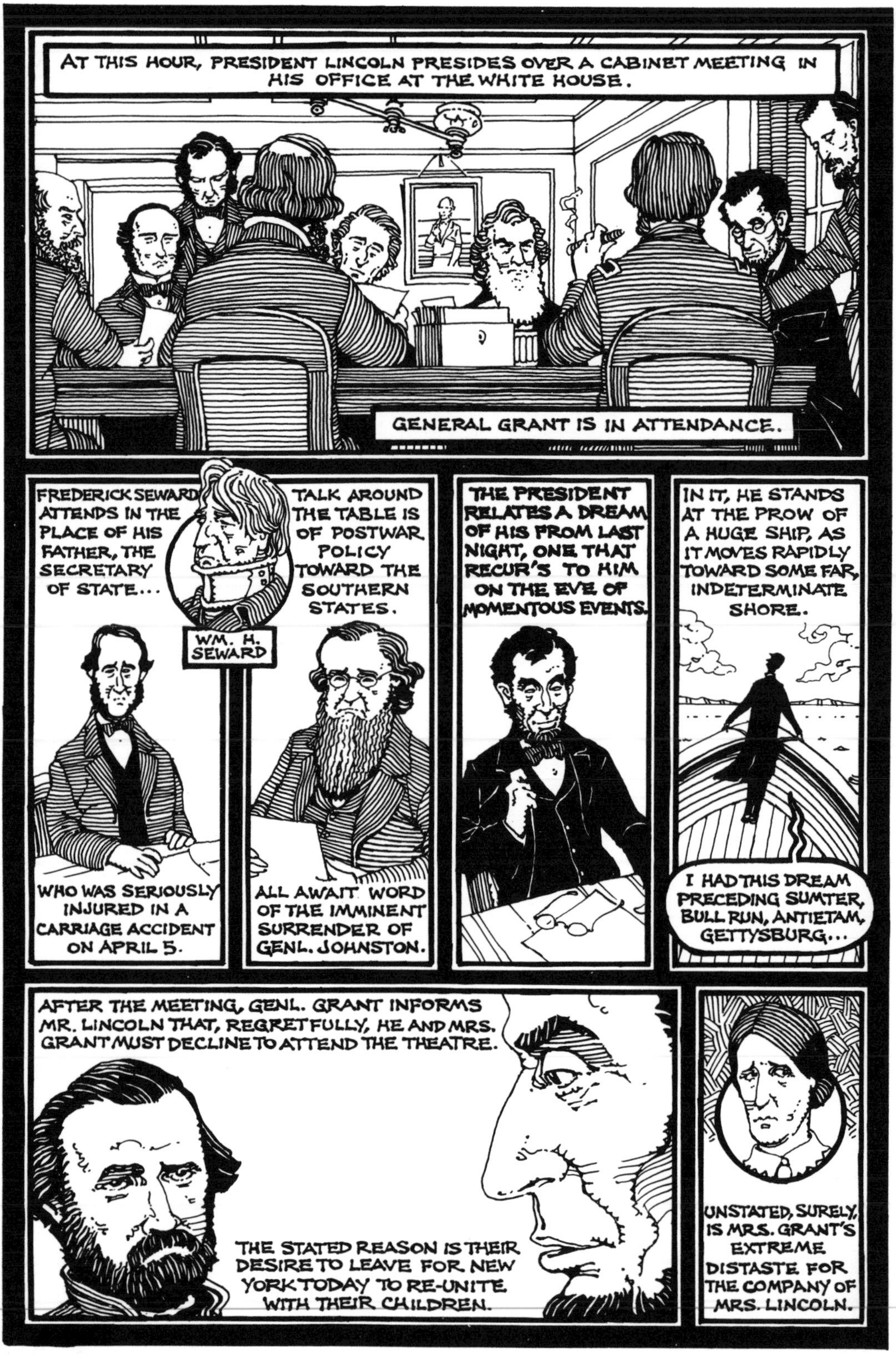
AT THIS HOUR, PRESIDENT LINCOLN PRESIDES OVER A CABINET MEETING IN HIS OFFICE AT THE WHITE HOUSE.
GENERAL GRANT IS IN ATTENDANCE.
FREDERICK SEWARD ATTENDS IN THE PLACE OF HIS FATHER, THE SECRETARY OF STATE...
WM. H. SEWARD
WHO WAS SERIOUSLY INJURED IN A CARRIAGE ACCIDENT ON APRIL 5.
TALK AROUND THE TABLE IS OF POSTWAR POLICY TOWARD THE SOUTHERN STATES.
ALL AWAIT WORD OF THE IMMINENT SURRENDER OF GENL. JOHNSTON.
THE PRESIDENT RELATES A DREAM OF HIS FROM LAST NIGHT, ONE THAT RECUR'S TO HIM ON THE EVE OF MOMENTOUS EVENTS.
IN IT, HE STANDS AT THE PROW OF A HUGE SHIP, AS IT MOVES RAPIDLY TOWARD SOME FAR, INDETERMINATE SHORE.
I HAD THIS DREAM PRECEDING SUMTER, BULL RUN, ANTIETAM, GETTYSBURG...
AFTER THE MEETING, GENL. GRANT INFORMS MR. LINCOLN THAT, REGRETFULLY, HE AND MRS. GRANT MUST DECLINE TO ATTEND THE THEATRE.
THE STATED REASON IS THEIR DESIRE TO LEAVE FOR NEW YORK TODAY TO RE-UNITE WITH THEIR CHILDREN.
UNSTATED, SURELY, IS MRS. GRANT'S EXTREME DISTASTE FOR THE COMPANY OF MRS. LINCOLN.

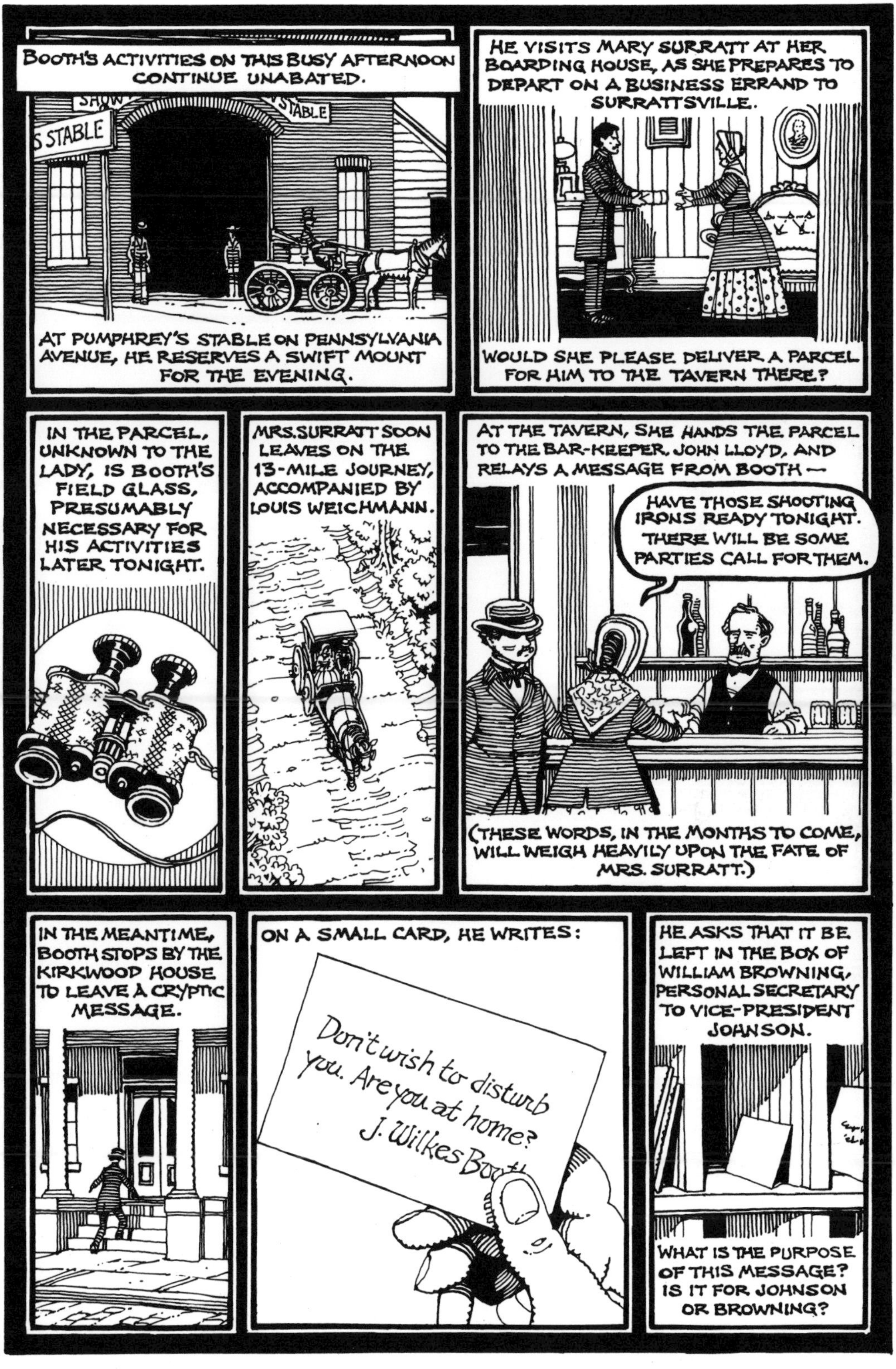
BOOTH'S ACTIVITIES ON THIS BUSY AFTERNOON CONTINUE UNABATED.
S STABLE
STABLE
AT PUMPHREY'S STABLE ON PENNSYLVANIA AVENUE, HE RESERVES A SWIFT MOUNT FOR THE EVENING.
HE VISITS MARY SURRATT AT HER BOARDING HOUSE, AS SHE PREPARES TO DEPART ON A BUSINESS ERRAND TO SURRATTSVILLE.
WOULD SHE PLEASE DELIVER A PARCEL FOR HIM TO THE TAVERN THERE?
IN THE PARCEL, UNKNOWN TO THE LADY, IS BOOTH'S FIELD GLASS, PRESUMABLY NECESSARY FOR HIS ACTIVITIES LATER TONIGHT.
MRS. SURRATT SOON LEAVES ON THE 13-MILE JOURNEY, ACCOMPANIED BY LOUIS WEICHMANN.
AT THE TAVERN, SHE HANDS THE PARCEL TO THE BAR-KEEPER, JOHN LLOYD, AND RELAYS A MESSAGE FROM BOOTH —
HAVE THOSE SHOOTING IRONS READY TONIGHT. THERE WILL BE SOME PARTIES CALL FOR THEM.
(THESE WORDS, IN THE MONTHS TO COME, WILL WEIGH HEAVILY UPON THE FATE OF MRS. SURRATT.)
IN THE MEANTIME, BOOTH STOPS BY THE KIRKWOOD HOUSE TO LEAVE A CRYPTIC MESSAGE.
ON A SMALL CARD, HE WRITES:
Don't wish to disturb you. Are you at home? J. Wilkes Booth
HE ASKS THAT IT BE LEFT IN THE BOX OF WILLIAM BROWNING, PERSONAL SECRETARY TO VICE-PRESIDENT JOHNSON.
WHAT IS THE PURPOSE OF THIS MESSAGE? IS IT FOR JOHNSON OR BROWNING?

AT THE WHITE HOUSE, THE CABINET MEETING, HAVING DRAGGED ON INTO MID-AFTERNOON, AT LAST CONCLUDES.

ACCOMPANIED BY HIS BODYGUARD, WM. CROOK, OF THE METROPOLITAN POLICE, LINCOLN WALKS NEXT DOOR TO THE WAR DEPARTMENT.

ON THE WALKWAY, WHICH IS OPEN TO THE PUBLIC, THEY PASS A GROUP OF DRUNKEN MEN.

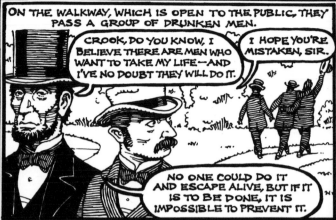

CROOK, DO YOU KNOW, I BELIEVE THERE ARE MEN WHO WANT TO TAKE MY LIFE—AND I'VE NO DOUBT THEY WILL DO IT.

I HOPE YOU'RE MISTAKEN, SIR.

NO ONE COULD DO IT AND ESCAPE ALIVE, BUT IF IT IS TO BE DONE, IT IS IMPOSSIBLE TO PREVENT IT.

AT THE OFFICE OF EDWIN M. STANTON, THE SECRETARY OF WAR, LINCOLN MAKES AN UNUSUAL REQUEST:

I AM LOOKING FOR SOMEONE TO GO TO THE THEATRE WITH ME TONIGHT. GRANT SAYS HE CANNOT ATTEND.

CAN I HAVE YOUR MAN ECKERT?

(HE REFERS TO MAJ. THOMAS ECKERT, THE BURLY CHIEF OF THE WAR DEPARTMENT'S TELEGRAPH OFFICE.)

I CANNOT SPARE HIM. I HAVE IMPORTANT WORK FOR HIM THIS EVENING.

WHY WOULD STANTON REFUSE THE PRESIDENT PROTECTION?

MORE IMPORTANTLY, WHY IS THE NOTORIOUSLY FATALISTIC PRESIDENT SO CONCERNED ABOUT HIS PERSONAL SAFETY ON THIS PARTICULAR EVENING?

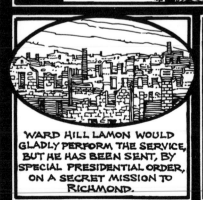

WARD HILL LAMON WOULD GLADLY PERFORM THE SERVICE, BUT HE HAS BEEN SENT, BY SPECIAL PRESIDENTIAL ORDER, ON A SECRET MISSION TO RICHMOND.

ON THE WALK BACK TO THE WHITE HOUSE, LINCOLN OFFERS CROOK A FURTHER CONFIDENCE...

HE HAS LITTLE INTEREST IN ATTENDING THE THEATRE TONIGHT, BUT FEELS HE MUST NOT DISAPPOINT THE PEOPLE.

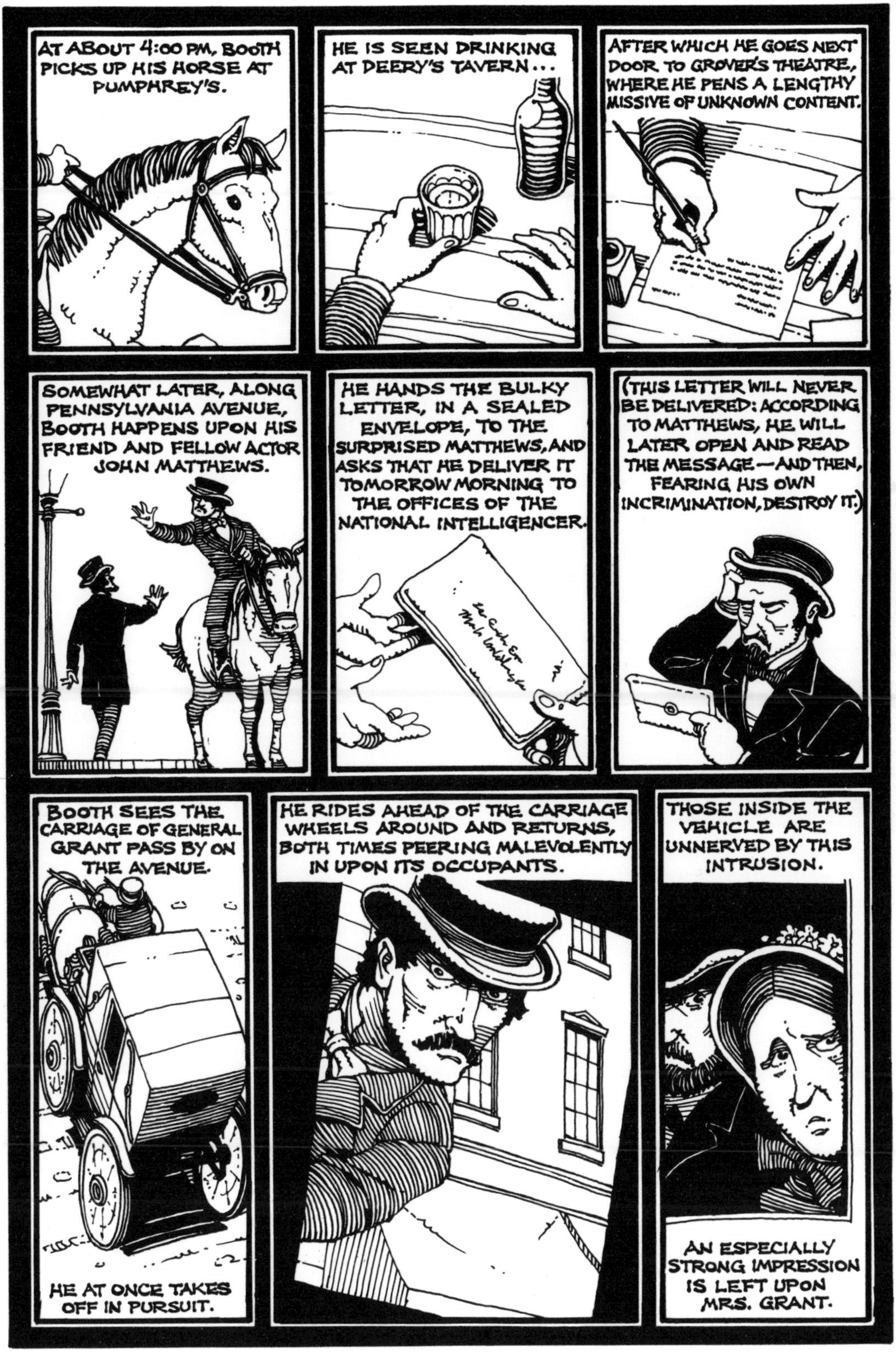
AT ABOUT 4:00 PM, BOOTH PICKS UP HIS HORSE AT PUMPHREY'S.
HE IS SEEN DRINKING AT DEERY'S TAVERN...
AFTER WHICH HE GOES NEXT DOOR TO GROVER'S THEATRE, WHERE HE PENS A LENGTHY MISSIVE OF UNKNOWN CONTENT.
SOMEWHAT LATER, ALONG PENNSYLVANIA AVENUE, BOOTH HAPPENS UPON HIS FRIEND AND FELLOW ACTOR JOHN MATTHEWS.
HE HANDS THE BULKY LETTER, IN A SEALED ENVELOPE, TO THE SURPRISED MATTHEWS, AND ASKS THAT HE DELIVER IT TOMORROW MORNING TO THE OFFICES OF THE NATIONAL INTELLIGENCER.
(THIS LETTER WILL NEVER BE DELIVERED: ACCORDING TO MATTHEWS, HE WILL LATER OPEN AND READ THE MESSAGE—AND THEN, FEARING HIS OWN INCRIMINATION, DESTROY IT.)
BOOTH SEES THE CARRIAGE OF GENERAL GRANT PASS BY ON THE AVENUE.
HE AT ONCE TAKES OFF IN PURSUIT.
HE RIDES AHEAD OF THE CARRIAGE WHEELS AROUND AND RETURNS, BOTH TIMES PEERING MALEVOLENTLY IN UPON ITS OCCUPANTS.
THOSE INSIDE THE VEHICLE ARE UNNERVED BY THIS INTRUSION.
AN ESPECIALLY STRONG IMPRESSION IS LEFT UPON MRS. GRANT.

BOOTH'S NEXT STOP, AT 5:30 OR 6:00 PM, IS FORD'S THEATRE, A BUILDING TO WHICH HE HAS UNLIMITED ACCESS.

AT THIS TIME OF THE AFTERNOON, REHEARSALS HAVING CONCLUDED, IT IS USUALLY EMPTY.

HE INVITES SOME OF THE STAGE HANDS FOR DRINKS AT TALTAVUL'S TAVERN NEXT DOOR.

HE THEN VENTURES UP TO THE DRESS CIRCLE AND AROUND TO THE PRESIDENTIAL BOX AND ITS OUTER VESTIBULE.

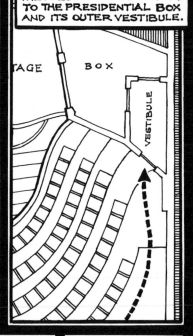

HE PROCURES A TWO-FOOT PINE BOARD (THE UPRIGHT PORTION OF A MUSIC-STAND) TO USE AS A BRACE FOR HOLDING SHUT THE OUTER DOOR...

CUTTING A SMALL NICHE INTO THE WALL TO SECURE IT.

HE THEN USES HIS PENKNIFE TO BORE A TINY HOLE IN THE INNER DOOR TO THE BOX...

THROUGH WHICH HE CAN VIEW THE OCCUPANTS AS THEY WATCH THE PLAY.

HIS PREPARATIONS COMPLETE, BOOTH RETURNS TO THE NATIONAL HOTEL FOR DINNER.

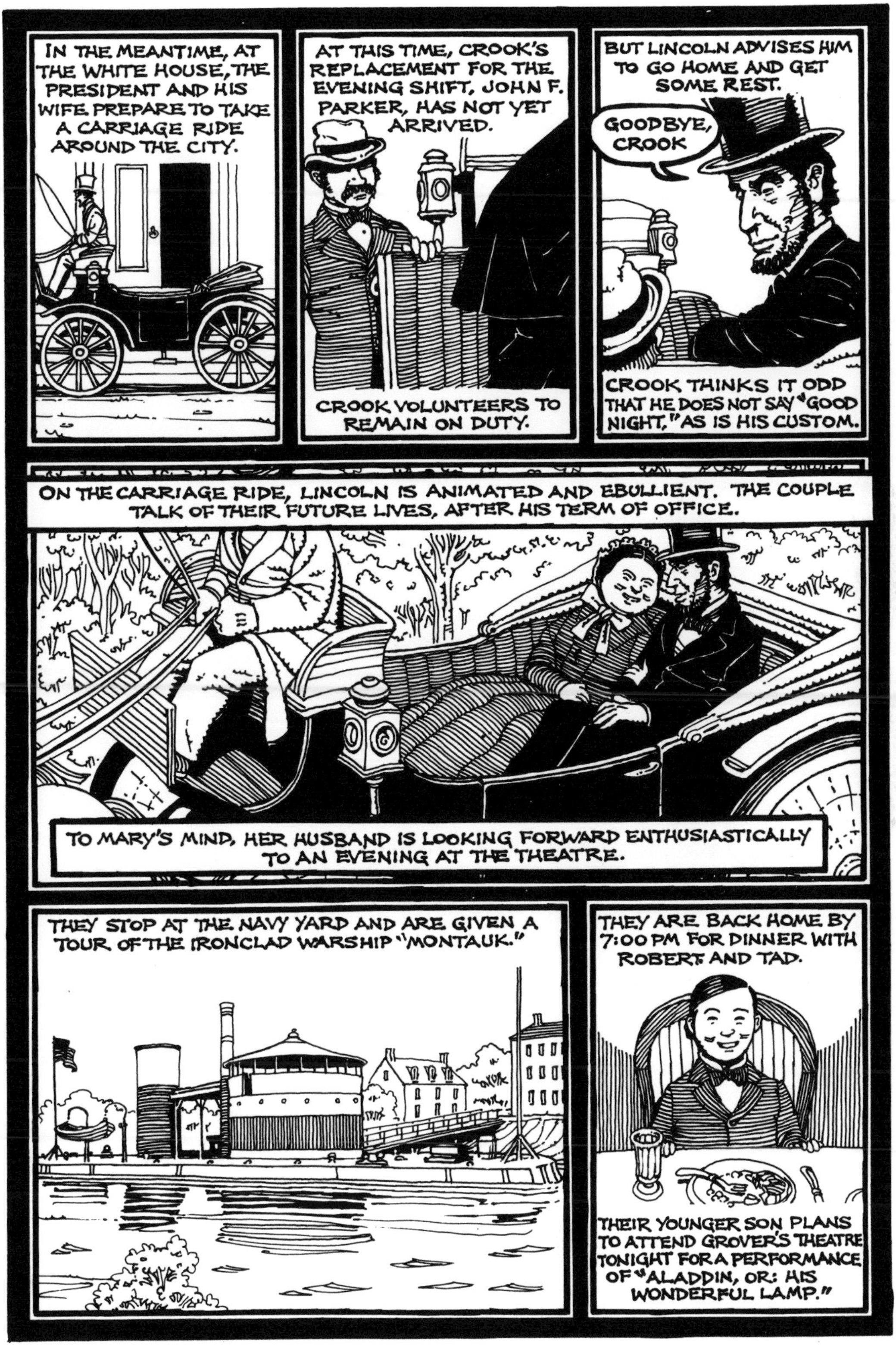
IN THE MEANTIME, AT THE WHITE HOUSE, THE PRESIDENT AND HIS WIFE PREPARE TO TAKE A CARRIAGE RIDE AROUND THE CITY.
AT THIS TIME, CROOK'S REPLACEMENT FOR THE EVENING SHIFT, JOHN F. PARKER, HAS NOT YET ARRIVED.
CROOK VOLUNTEERS TO REMAIN ON DUTY.
BUT LINCOLN ADVISES HIM TO GO HOME AND GET SOME REST.
GOODBYE, CROOK
CROOK THINKS IT ODD THAT HE DOES NOT SAY "GOOD NIGHT," AS IS HIS CUSTOM.
ON THE CARRIAGE RIDE, LINCOLN IS ANIMATED AND EBULLIENT. THE COUPLE TALK OF THEIR FUTURE LIVES, AFTER HIS TERM OF OFFICE.
TO MARY'S MIND, HER HUSBAND IS LOOKING FORWARD ENTHUSIASTICALLY TO AN EVENING AT THE THEATRE.
THEY STOP AT THE NAVY YARD AND ARE GIVEN A TOUR OF THE IRONCLAD WARSHIP "MONTAUK."
THEY ARE BACK HOME BY 7:00 PM FOR DINNER WITH ROBERT AND TAD.
THEIR YOUNGER SON PLANS TO ATTEND GROVER'S THEATRE TONIGHT FOR A PERFORMANCE OF "ALADDIN, OR: HIS WONDERFUL LAMP."

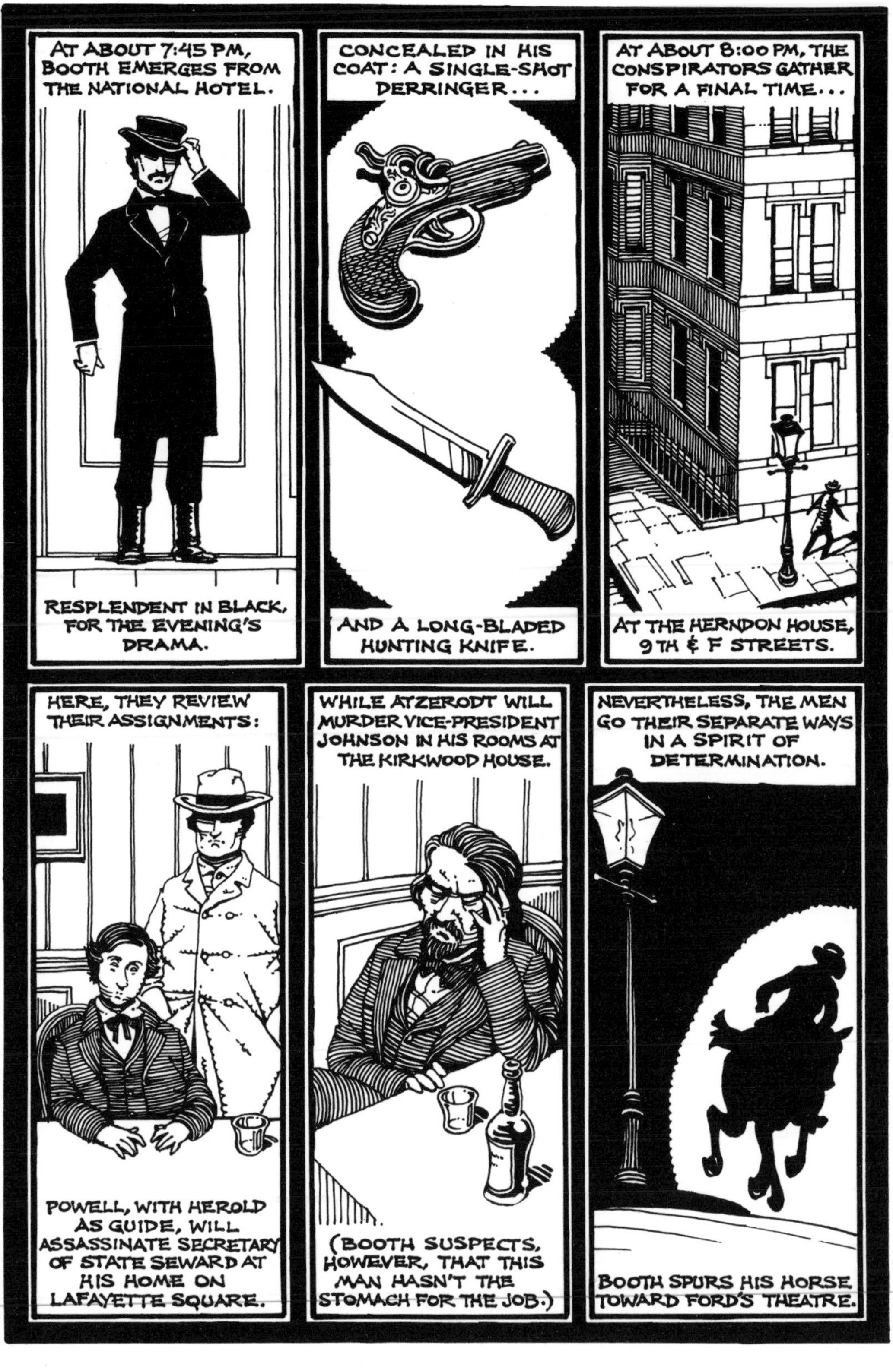
AT ABOUT 7:45 PM, BOOTH EMERGES FROM THE NATIONAL HOTEL.
RESPLENDENT IN BLACK, FOR THE EVENING'S DRAMA.
CONCEALED IN HIS COAT: A SINGLE-SHOT DERRINGER...
AND A LONG-BLADED HUNTING KNIFE.
AT ABOUT 8:00 PM, THE CONSPIRATORS GATHER FOR A FINAL TIME...
AT THE HERNDON HOUSE, 9TH & F STREETS.
HERE, THEY REVIEW THEIR ASSIGNMENTS:
POWELL, WITH HEROLD AS GUIDE, WILL ASSASSINATE SECRETARY OF STATE SEWARD AT HIS HOME ON LAFAYETTE SQUARE.
WHILE ATZERODT WILL MURDER VICE-PRESIDENT JOHNSON IN HIS ROOMS AT THE KIRKWOOD HOUSE.
(BOOTH SUSPECTS, HOWEVER, THAT THIS MAN HASN'T THE STOMACH FOR THE JOB.)
NEVERTHELESS, THE MEN GO THEIR SEPARATE WAYS IN A SPIRIT OF DETERMINATION.
BOOTH SPURS HIS HORSE TOWARD FORD'S THEATRE.

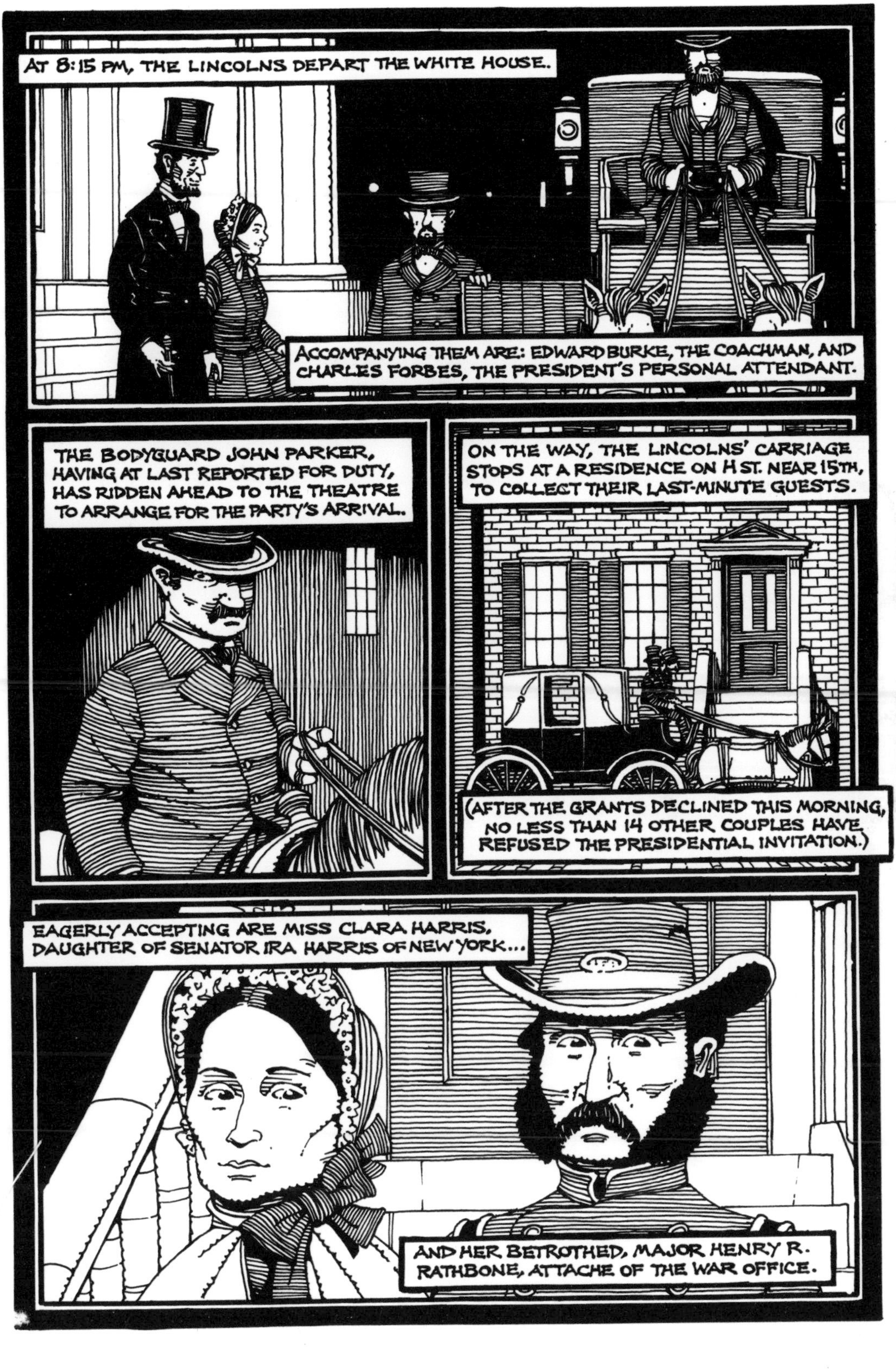
AT 8:15 PM, THE LINCOLNS DEPART THE WHITE HOUSE.
ACCOMPANYING THEM ARE: EDWARD BURKE, THE COACHMAN, AND CHARLES FORBES, THE PRESIDENT'S PERSONAL ATTENDANT.
THE BODYGUARD JOHN PARKER, HAVING AT LAST REPORTED FOR DUTY, HAS RIDDEN AHEAD TO THE THEATRE TO ARRANGE FOR THE PARTY'S ARRIVAL.
ON THE WAY, THE LINCOLNS' CARRIAGE STOPS AT A RESIDENCE ON H ST. NEAR 15TH, TO COLLECT THEIR LAST-MINUTE GUESTS.
(AFTER THE GRANTS DECLINED THIS MORNING, NO LESS THAN 14 OTHER COUPLES HAVE REFUSED THE PRESIDENTIAL INVITATION.)
EAGERLY ACCEPTING ARE MISS CLARA HARRIS, DAUGHTER OF SENATOR IRA HARRIS OF NEW YORK...
AND HER BETROTHED, MAJOR HENRY R. RATHBONE, ATTACHE OF THE WAR OFFICE.

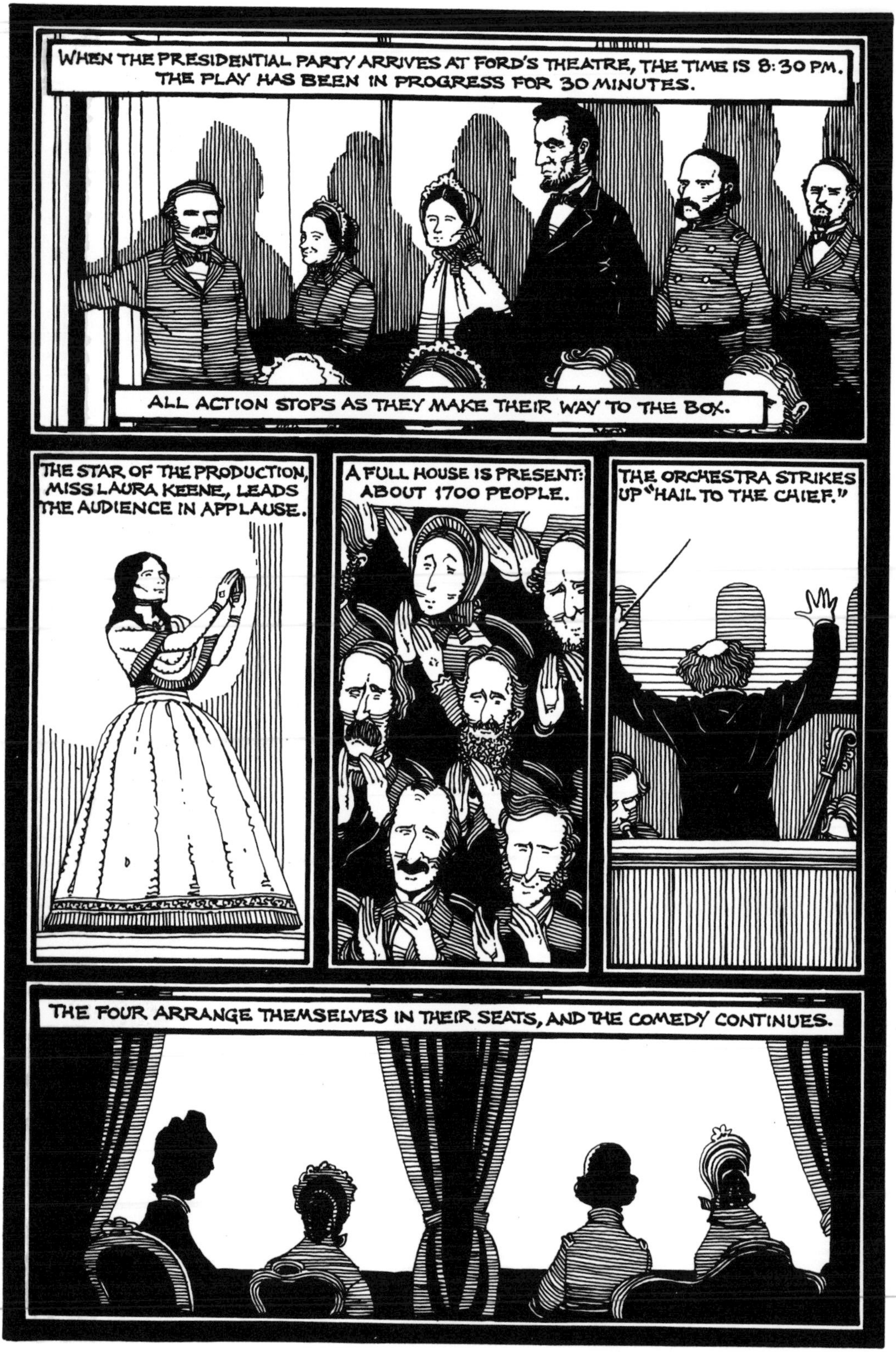
WHEN THE PRESIDENTIAL PARTY ARRIVES AT FORD'S THEATRE, THE TIME IS 8:30 PM. THE PLAY HAS BEEN IN PROGRESS FOR 30 MINUTES.
ALL ACTION STOPS AS THEY MAKE THEIR WAY TO THE BOX.
THE STAR OF THE PRODUCTION, MISS LAURA KEENE, LEADS THE AUDIENCE IN APPLAUSE.
A FULL HOUSE IS PRESENT: ABOUT 1700 PEOPLE.
THE ORCHESTRA STRIKES UP "HAIL TO THE CHIEF."
THE FOUR ARRANGE THEMSELVES IN THEIR SEATS, AND THE COMEDY CONTINUES.

AT 9:30 PM, BOOTH DISMOUNTS IN THE ALLEY BEHIND THE THEATRE.

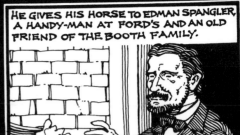

HE GIVES HIS HORSE TO EDMAN SPANGLER, A HANDY-MAN AT FORD'S AND AN OLD FRIEND OF THE BOOTH FAMILY.

THE ACTOR SAYS HE WILL RETURN SHORTLY.

AFTER BOOTH ENTERS THE THEATRE, SPANGLER, NEEDING TO RESUME HIS DUTIES, RECRUITS A YOUNG MAN NAMED JOSEPH BURROUGHS (KNOWN AS "JOHN PEANUT") TO MIND THE ANIMAL.

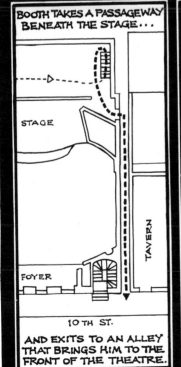

BOOTH TAKES A PASSAGEWAY BENEATH THE STAGE...

STAGE

FOYER

TAVERN

10TH ST.

AND EXITS TO AN ALLEY THAT BRINGS HIM TO THE FRONT OF THE THEATRE.

HE IS SEEN BY THE TICKET-SELLER NERVOUSLY ENTERING AND RE-ENTERING THE FOYER.

HE ORDERS BRANDY AT TALTAVUL'S NEXT DOOR.

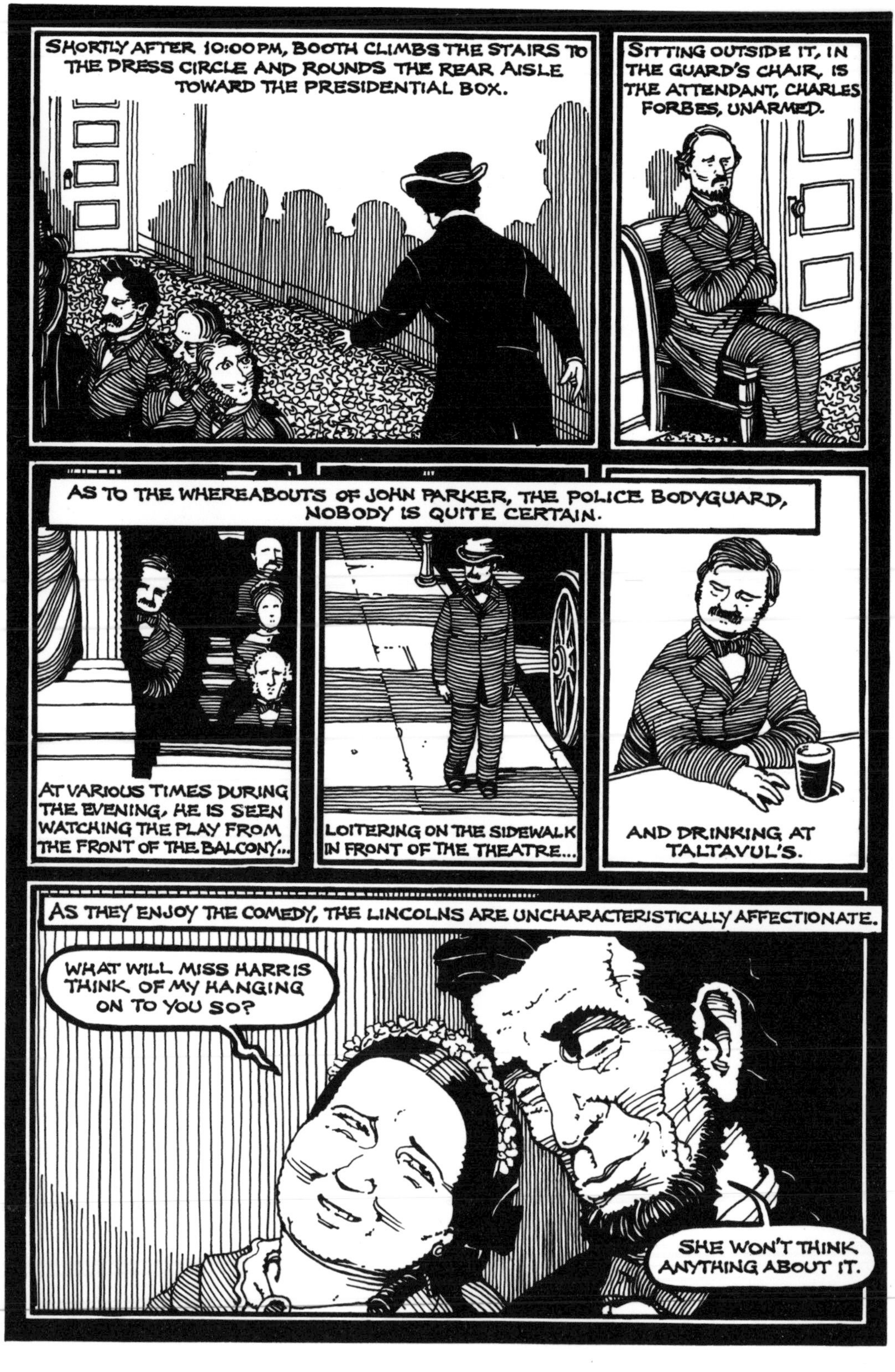
SHORTLY AFTER 10:00 PM, BOOTH CLIMBS THE STAIRS TO THE DRESS CIRCLE AND ROUNDS THE REAR AISLE TOWARD THE PRESIDENTIAL BOX.
SITTING OUTSIDE IT, IN THE GUARD'S CHAIR, IS THE ATTENDANT, CHARLES FORBES, UNARMED.
AS TO THE WHEREABOUTS OF JOHN PARKER, THE POLICE BODYGUARD, NOBODY IS QUITE CERTAIN.
AT VARIOUS TIMES DURING THE EVENING, HE IS SEEN WATCHING THE PLAY FROM THE FRONT OF THE BALCONY...
LOITERING ON THE SIDEWALK IN FRONT OF THE THEATRE...
AND DRINKING AT TALTAVUL'S.
AS THEY ENJOY THE COMEDY, THE LINCOLNS ARE UNCHARACTERISTICALLY AFFECTIONATE.
WHAT WILL MISS HARRIS THINK OF MY HANGING ON TO YOU SO?
SHE WON'T THINK ANYTHING ABOUT IT.

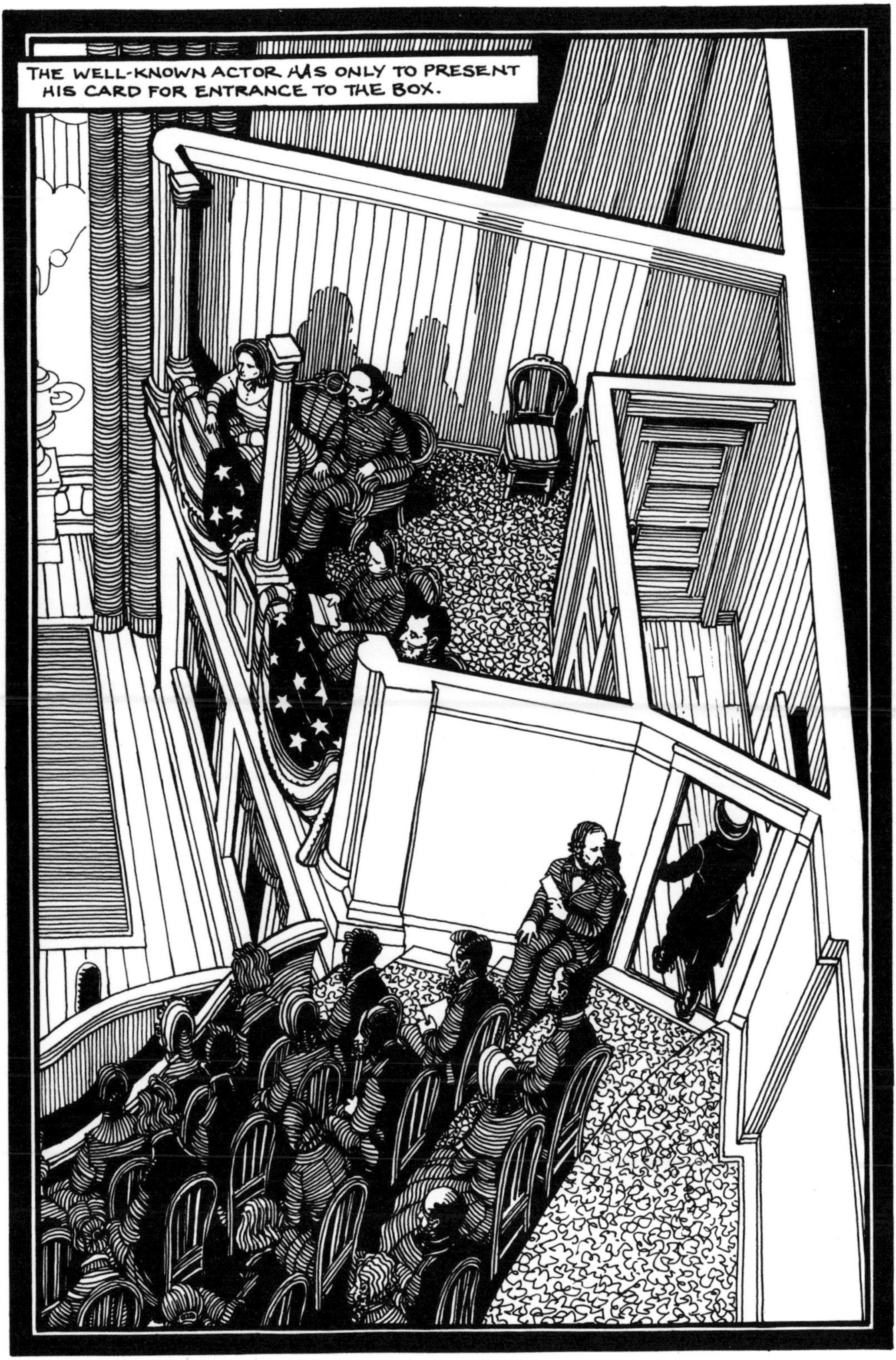
THE WELL-KNOWN ACTOR HAS ONLY TO PRESENT HIS CARD FOR ENTRANCE TO THE BOX.

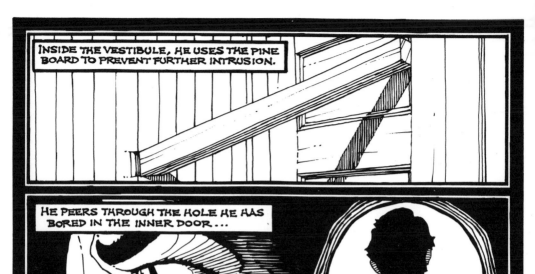

INSIDE THE VESTIBULE, HE USES THE PINE BOARD TO PREVENT FURTHER INTRUSION.

HE PEERS THROUGH THE HOLE HE HAS BORED IN THE INNER DOOR...

AND SIGHTS HIS TARGET.

AT ABOUT 10:15 PM, HE SLOWLY PUSHES THE DOOR OPEN—AND AWAITS THE CRUCIAL MOMENT.

IT IS ACT III, SCENE 2, AND THE SINGLE ACTOR ONSTAGE (HARRY HAWK AS "ASA TRENCHARD") DELIVERS A LINE THAT NEVER FAILS TO BRING UPROARIOUS LAUGHTER.

DON'T KNOW THE MANNERS OF GOOD SOCIETY, EH? WELL, I GUESS I KNOW ENOUGH TO TURN YOU INSIDE OUT, OLD GAL— YOU SOCKDOLOGIZING OLD MAN TRAP!

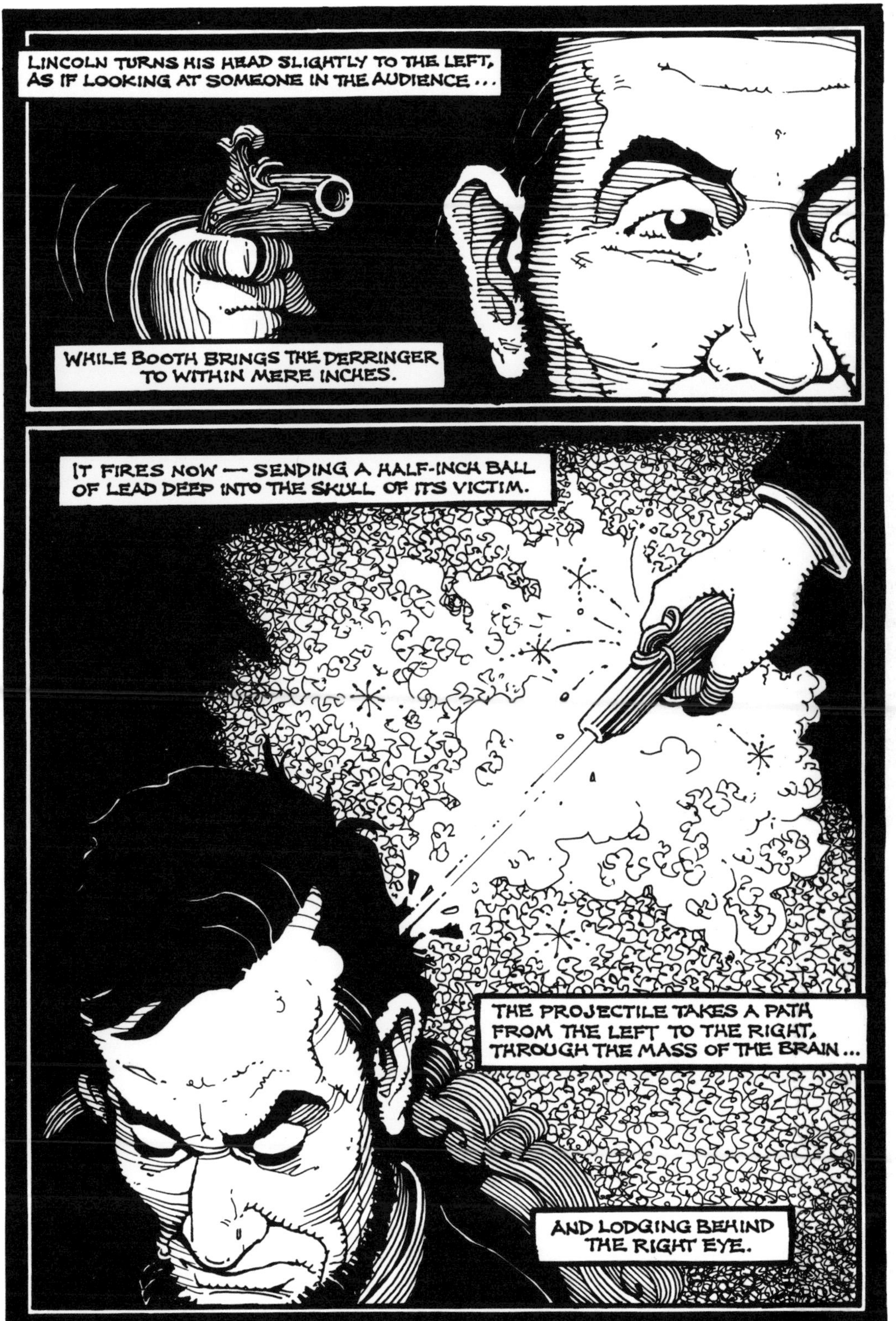
LINCOLN TURNS HIS HEAD SLIGHTLY TO THE LEFT, AS IF LOOKING AT SOMEONE IN THE AUDIENCE . . .
WHILE BOOTH BRINGS THE DERRINGER TO WITHIN MERE INCHES.
IT FIRES NOW — SENDING A HALF-INCH BALL OF LEAD DEEP INTO THE SKULL OF ITS VICTIM.
THE PROJECTILE TAKES A PATH FROM THE LEFT TO THE RIGHT, THROUGH THE MASS OF THE BRAIN . . .
AND LODGING BEHIND THE RIGHT EYE.

FOR ONE HORRIBLE MOMENT, THE THEATRE IS SUSPENDED IN A BREATHLESS SILENCE.

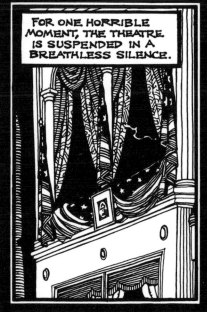

THE PRESIDENT, HAVING LOST ALL MOTOR FUNCTION, SLUMPS FORWARD IN HIS ROCKER.

HIS STILL-BEWILDERED WIFE ATTEMPTS TO KEEP HIM UPRIGHT.

BOOTH DROPS THE PISTOL AND MAKES FOR THE RAILING OF THE BOX. MAJOR RATHBONE LEAPS INTO ACTION, LUNGING AT THE ASSAILANT...

ONLY TO RECEIVE A VICIOUS GASH TO HIS ARM FROM THE ASSASSIN'S BLADE.

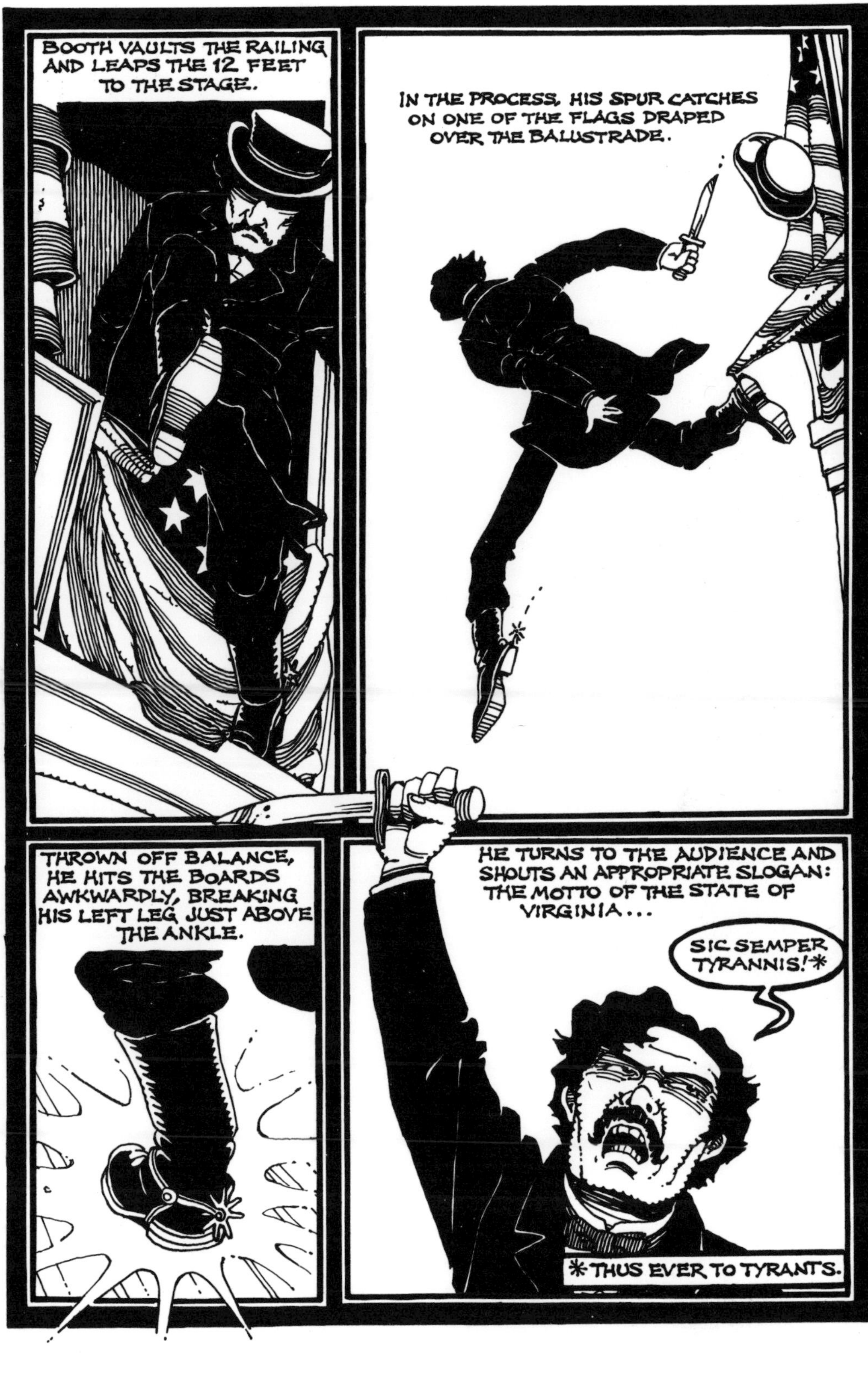
BOOTH VAULTS THE RAILING AND LEAPS THE 12 FEET TO THE STAGE.
IN THE PROCESS, HIS SPUR CATCHES ON ONE OF THE FLAGS DRAPED OVER THE BALUSTRADE.
THROWN OFF BALANCE, HE HITS THE BOARDS AWKWARDLY, BREAKING HIS LEFT LEG JUST ABOVE THE ANKLE.
HE TURNS TO THE AUDIENCE AND SHOUTS AN APPROPRIATE SLOGAN: THE MOTTO OF THE STATE OF VIRGINIA...
SIC SEMPER TYRANNIS!*
*THUS EVER TO TYRANTS.

A SCREAM ISSUES FROM THE PRESIDENTIAL BOX...

AND THE THEATRE AWAKENS TO WHAT IS HAPPENING.

BOOTH LIMPS ACROSS THE STAGE, TOWARD THE REAR DOOR THROUGH WHICH HE ENTERED...

THREATENING ANY WHO STAND IN HIS WAY.

IN THE ALLEY, HE GRABS THE REINS FROM YOUNG BURROUGHS...

GIVING THE LAD A VIOLENT KICK FOR GOOD MEASURE.

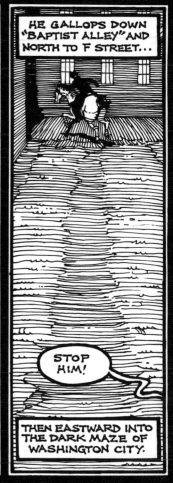

HE GALLOPS DOWN "BAPTIST ALLEY" AND NORTH TO F STREET...

STOP HIM!

THEN EASTWARD INTO THE DARK MAZE OF WASHINGTON CITY.

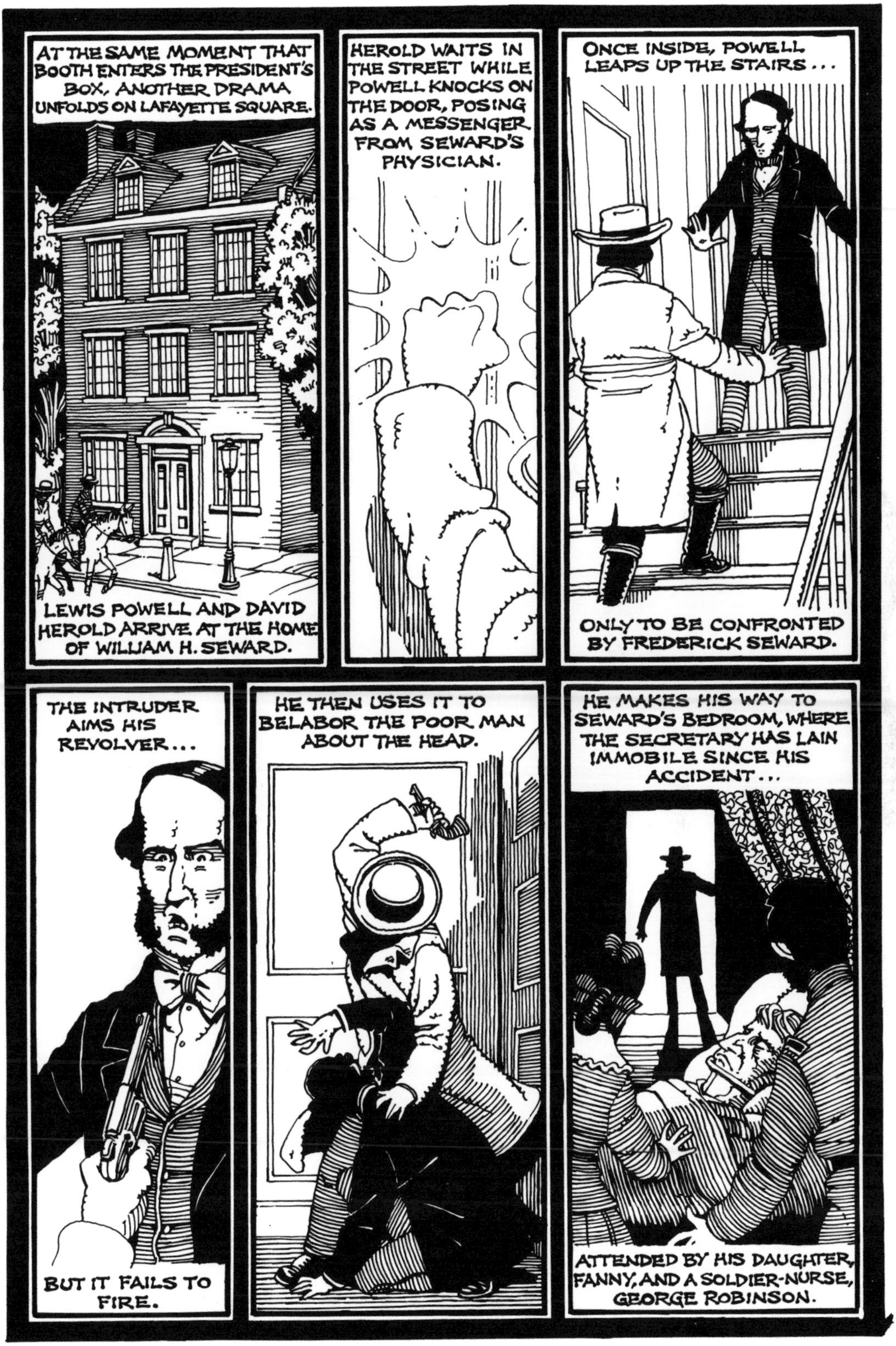
AT THE SAME MOMENT THAT BOOTH ENTERS THE PRESIDENT'S BOX, ANOTHER DRAMA UNFOLDS ON LAFAYETTE SQUARE.
LEWIS POWELL AND DAVID HEROLD ARRIVE AT THE HOME OF WILLIAM H. SEWARD.
HEROLD WAITS IN THE STREET WHILE POWELL KNOCKS ON THE DOOR, POSING AS A MESSENGER FROM SEWARD'S PHYSICIAN.
ONCE INSIDE, POWELL LEAPS UP THE STAIRS . . .
ONLY TO BE CONFRONTED BY FREDERICK SEWARD.
THE INTRUDER AIMS HIS REVOLVER . . .
BUT IT FAILS TO FIRE.
HE THEN USES IT TO BELABOR THE POOR MAN ABOUT THE HEAD.
HE MAKES HIS WAY TO SEWARD'S BEDROOM, WHERE THE SECRETARY HAS LAIN IMMOBILE SINCE HIS ACCIDENT . . .
ATTENDED BY HIS DAUGHTER, FANNY, AND A SOLDIER-NURSE, GEORGE ROBINSON.

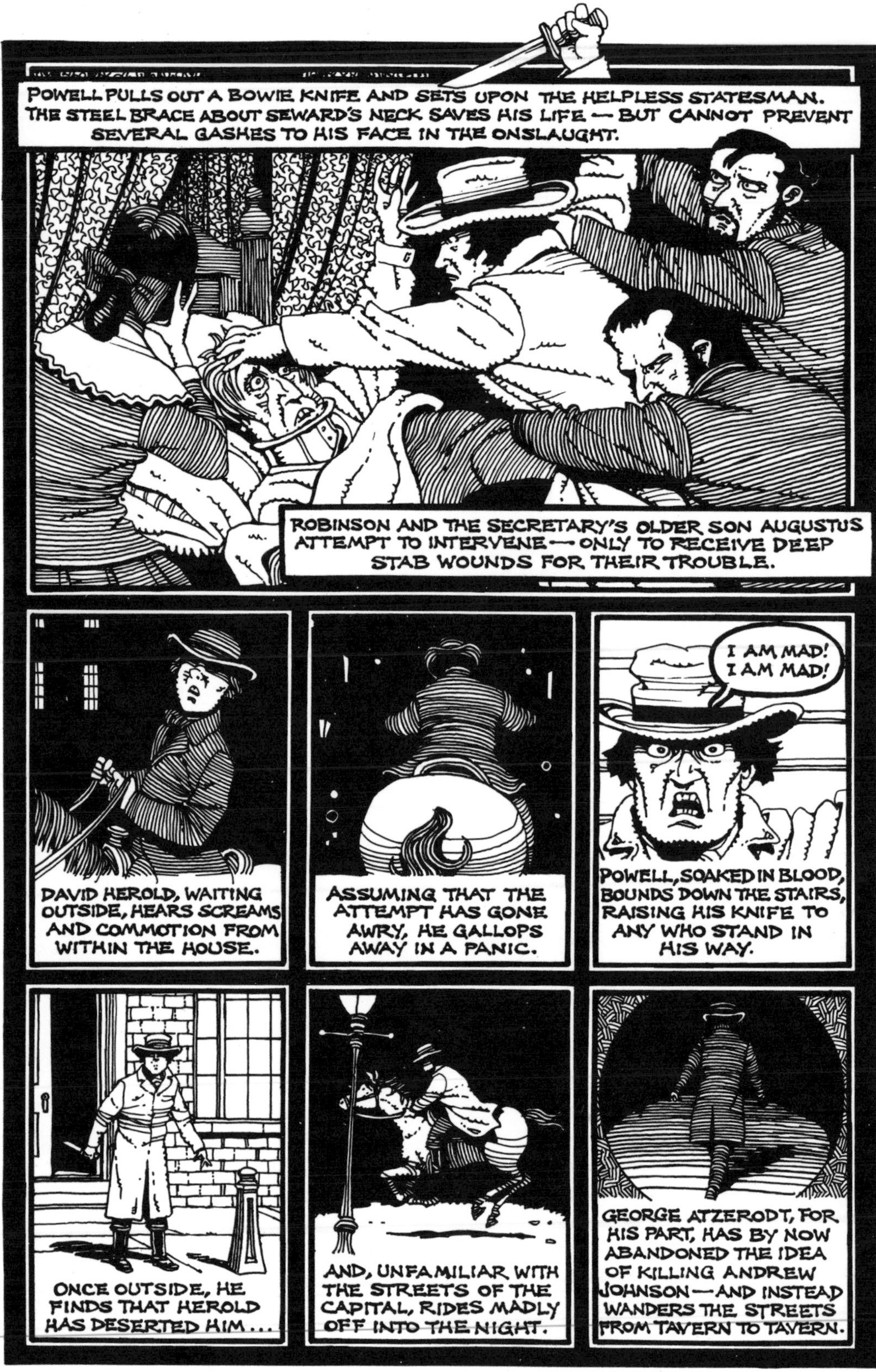
POWELL PULLS OUT A BOWIE KNIFE AND SETS UPON THE HELPLESS STATESMAN. THE STEEL BRACE ABOUT SEWARD'S NECK SAVES HIS LIFE — BUT CANNOT PREVENT SEVERAL GASHES TO HIS FACE IN THE ONSLAUGHT.
ROBINSON AND THE SECRETARY'S OLDER SON AUGUSTUS ATTEMPT TO INTERVENE — ONLY TO RECEIVE DEEP STAB WOUNDS FOR THEIR TROUBLE.
DAVID HEROLD, WAITING OUTSIDE, HEARS SCREAMS AND COMMOTION FROM WITHIN THE HOUSE.
ASSUMING THAT THE ATTEMPT HAS GONE AWRY, HE GALLOPS AWAY IN A PANIC.
I AM MAD! I AM MAD!
POWELL, SOAKED IN BLOOD, BOUNDS DOWN THE STAIRS, RAISING HIS KNIFE TO ANY WHO STAND IN HIS WAY.
ONCE OUTSIDE, HE FINDS THAT HEROLD HAS DESERTED HIM...
AND, UNFAMILIAR WITH THE STREETS OF THE CAPITAL, RIDES MADLY OFF INTO THE NIGHT.
GEORGE ATZERODT, FOR HIS PART, HAS BY NOW ABANDONED THE IDEA OF KILLING ANDREW JOHNSON — AND INSTEAD WANDERS THE STREETS FROM TAVERN TO TAVERN.

BACK AT FORD'S THEATRE, CHAOS AND CONFUSION DOMINATE.

MISS HARRIS CALLS FOR WATER ... AND A DOCTOR.

RATHBONE RECOVERS HIS SENSES ENOUGH TO REMOVE THE BOARD SECURING THE OUTER DOOR.

THE FIRST DOCTOR INTO THE BOX IS CHARLES LEALE, AGE 23. THE SECOND IS CHARLES TAFT, ALSO 23. TOGETHER, THEY GENTLY MOVE THE PRESIDENT ONTO THE FLOOR.

LEALE FINDS AND PROBES THE WOUND. HE SEES LITTLE REASON FOR HOPE.

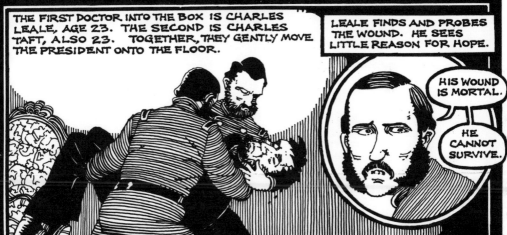

HIS WOUND IS MORTAL.

HE CANNOT SURVIVE.

NEVERTHELESS, HE STILL BREATHES SHALLOWLY, AND A FAINT HEARTBEAT CAN BE MEASURED.

MISS LAURA KEENE SOMEHOW MAKES HER WAY INTO THE BOX. SHE CRADLES LINCOLN'S HEAD IN HER LAP.

MARY LINCOLN, SOBBING UNCONTROLABLY, PAYS HER NO ATTENTION.

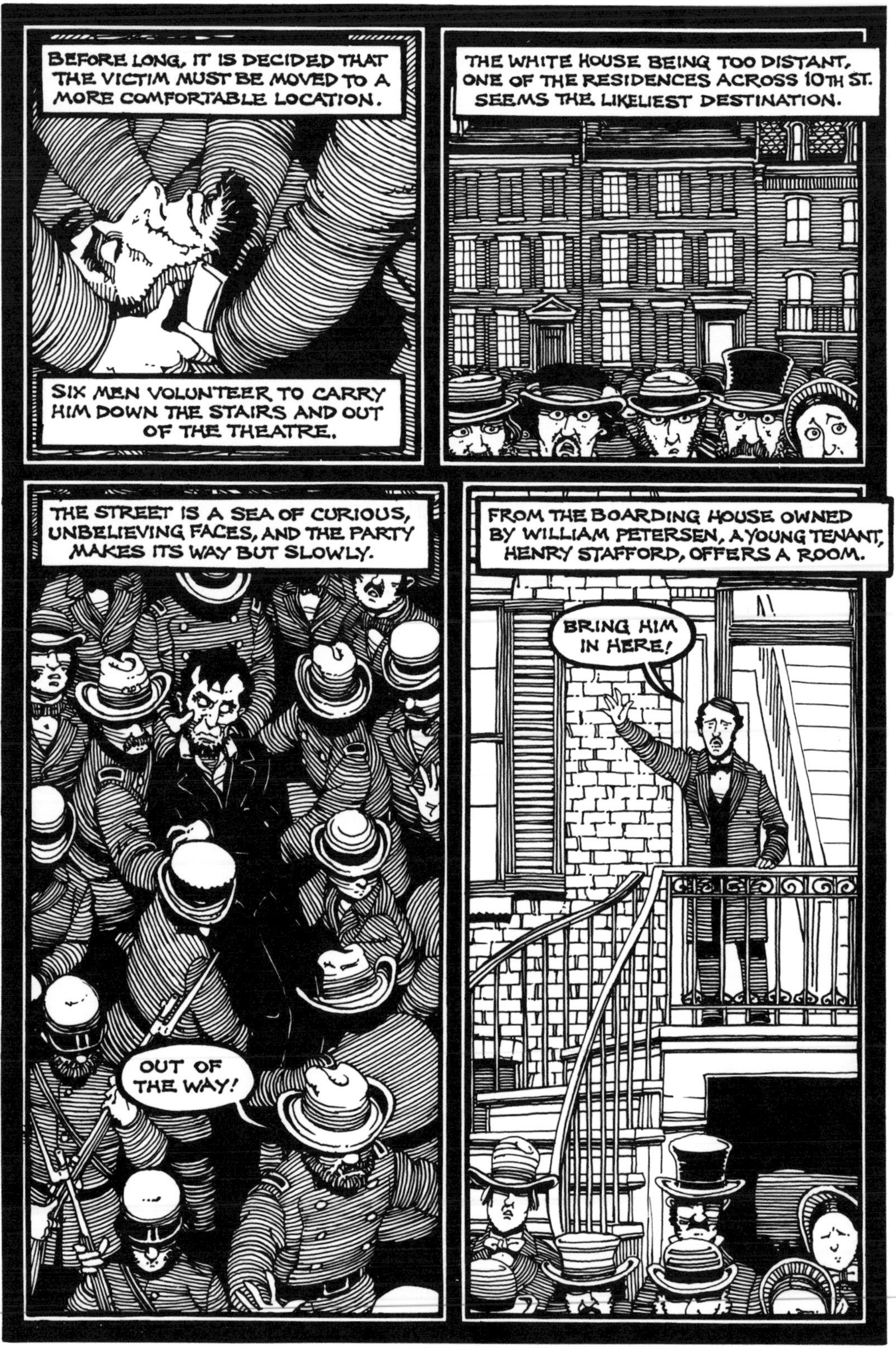
BEFORE LONG, IT IS DECIDED THAT THE VICTIM MUST BE MOVED TO A MORE COMFORTABLE LOCATION.
SIX MEN VOLUNTEER TO CARRY HIM DOWN THE STAIRS AND OUT OF THE THEATRE.
THE WHITE HOUSE BEING TOO DISTANT, ONE OF THE RESIDENCES ACROSS 10TH ST. SEEMS THE LIKELIEST DESTINATION.
THE STREET IS A SEA OF CURIOUS, UNBELIEVING FACES, AND THE PARTY MAKES ITS WAY BUT SLOWLY.
OUT OF THE WAY!
...
FROM THE BOARDING HOUSE OWNED BY WILLIAM PETERSEN, A YOUNG TENANT, HENRY STAFFORD, OFFERS A ROOM.
BRING HIM IN HERE!

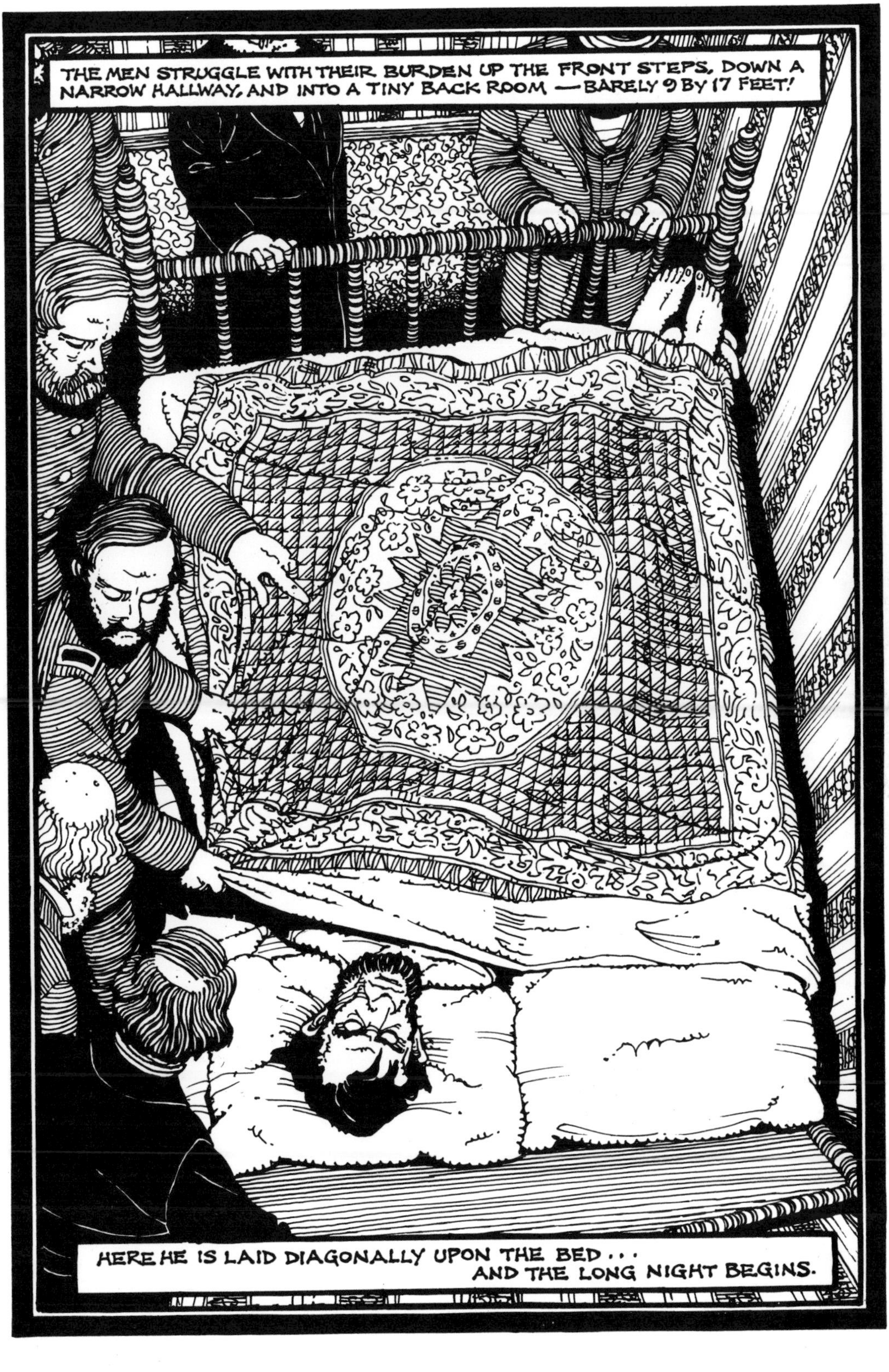
THE MEN STRUGGLE WITH THEIR BURDEN UP THE FRONT STEPS, DOWN A NARROW HALLWAY, AND INTO A TINY BACK ROOM — BARELY 9 BY 17 FEET!
HERE HE IS LAID DIAGONALLY UPON THE BED . . . AND THE LONG NIGHT BEGINS.

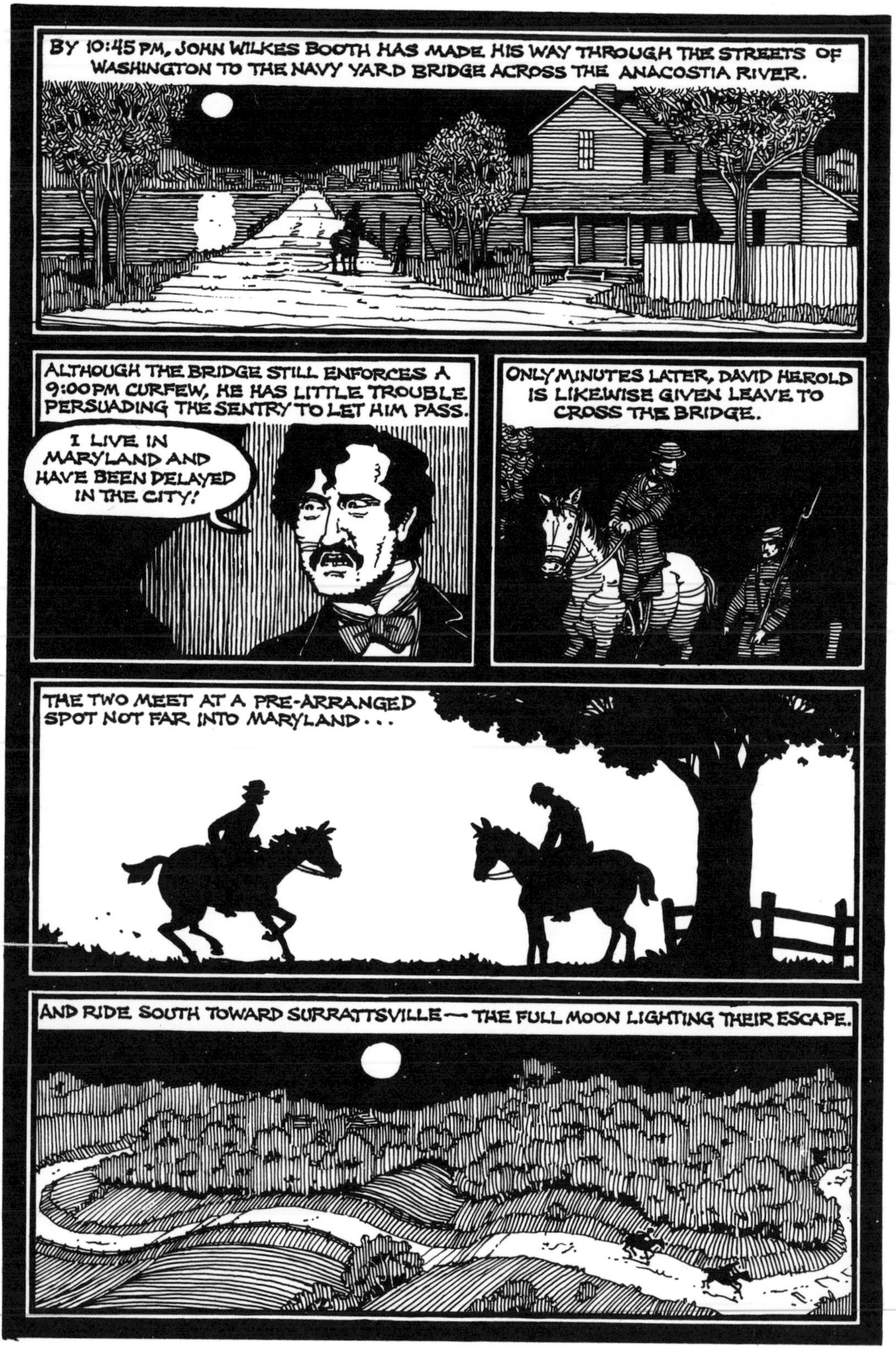
BY 10:45 PM, JOHN WILKES BOOTH HAS MADE HIS WAY THROUGH THE STREETS OF WASHINGTON TO THE NAVY YARD BRIDGE ACROSS THE ANACOSTIA RIVER.
ALTHOUGH THE BRIDGE STILL ENFORCES A 9:00PM CURFEW, HE HAS LITTLE TROUBLE PERSUADING THE SENTRY TO LET HIM PASS.
I LIVE IN MARYLAND AND HAVE BEEN DELAYED IN THE CITY!
ONLY MINUTES LATER, DAVID HEROLD IS LIKEWISE GIVEN LEAVE TO CROSS THE BRIDGE.
THE TWO MEET AT A PRE-ARRANGED SPOT NOT FAR INTO MARYLAND . . .
AND RIDE SOUTH TOWARD SURRATTSVILLE — THE FULL MOON LIGHTING THEIR ESCAPE.

PART IV.

THE ESCAPE

THE GARRETT FARM

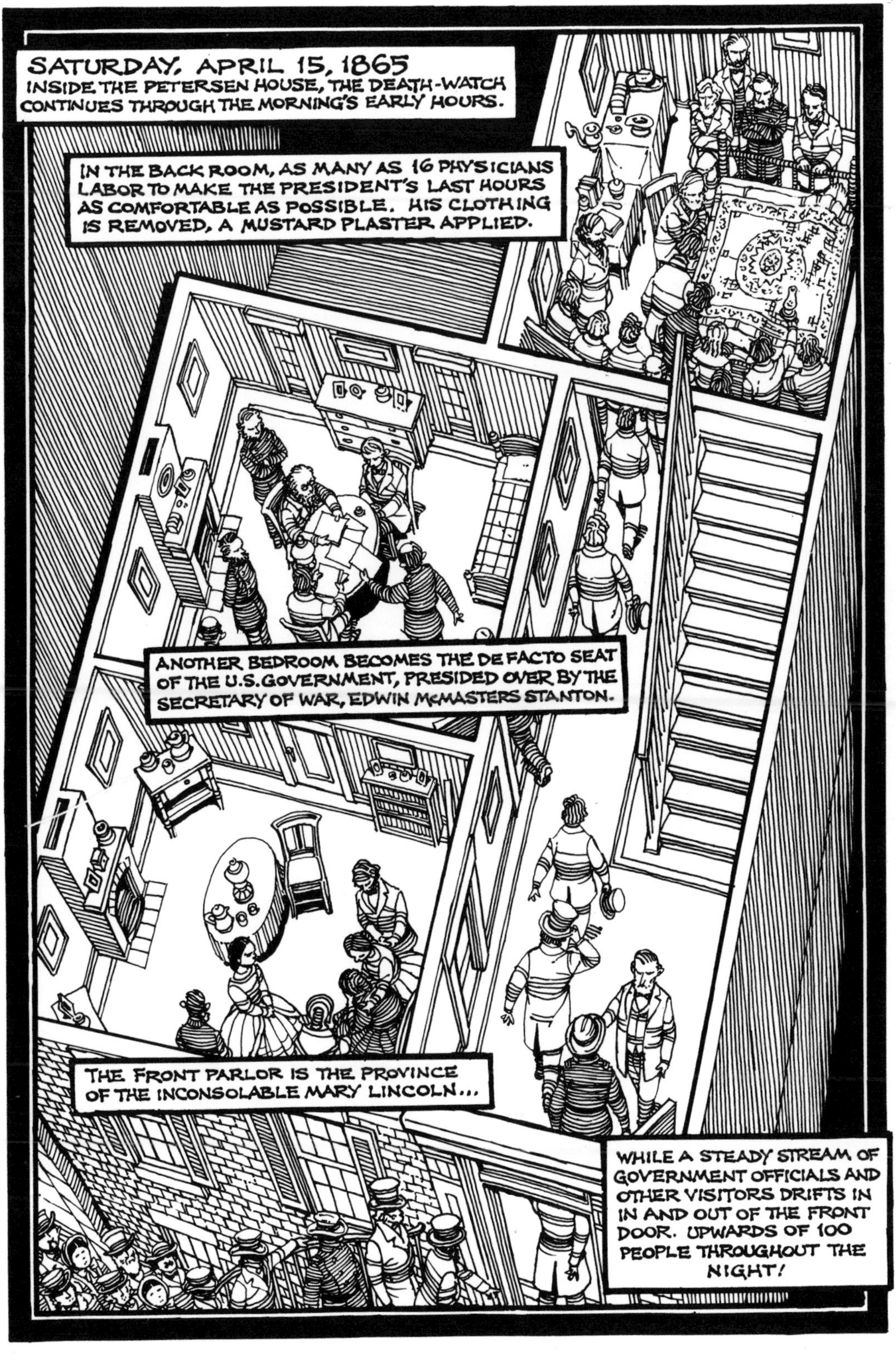
SATURDAY, APRIL 15, 1865
INSIDE THE PETERSEN HOUSE, THE DEATH-WATCH CONTINUES THROUGH THE MORNING'S EARLY HOURS.
IN THE BACK ROOM, AS MANY AS 16 PHYSICIANS LABOR TO MAKE THE PRESIDENT'S LAST HOURS AS COMFORTABLE AS POSSIBLE. HIS CLOTHING IS REMOVED, A MUSTARD PLASTER APPLIED.
ANOTHER BEDROOM BECOMES THE DE FACTO SEAT OF THE U.S. GOVERNMENT, PRESIDED OVER BY THE SECRETARY OF WAR, EDWIN McMASTERS STANTON.
THE FRONT PARLOR IS THE PROVINCE OF THE INCONSOLABLE MARY LINCOLN...
WHILE A STEADY STREAM OF GOVERNMENT OFFICIALS AND OTHER VISITORS DRIFTS IN IN AND OUT OF THE FRONT DOOR. UPWARDS OF 100 PEOPLE THROUGHOUT THE NIGHT!

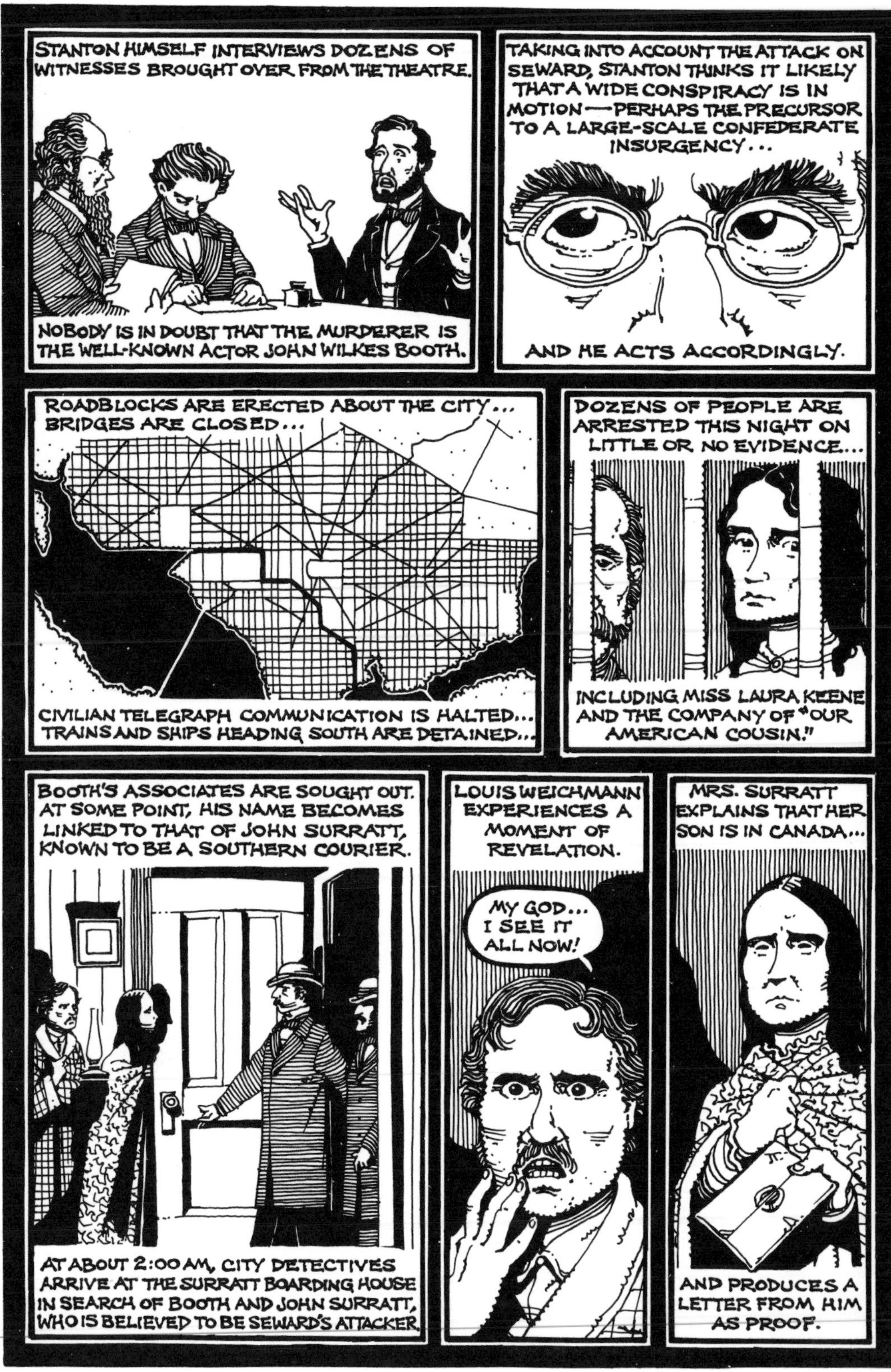
STANTON HIMSELF INTERVIEWS DOZENS OF WITNESSES BROUGHT OVER FROM THE THEATRE.
NOBODY IS IN DOUBT THAT THE MURDERER IS THE WELL-KNOWN ACTOR JOHN WILKES BOOTH.
TAKING INTO ACCOUNT THE ATTACK ON SEWARD, STANTON THINKS IT LIKELY THAT A WIDE CONSPIRACY IS IN MOTION — PERHAPS THE PRECURSOR TO A LARGE-SCALE CONFEDERATE INSURGENCY...
AND HE ACTS ACCORDINGLY.
ROADBLOCKS ARE ERECTED ABOUT THE CITY... BRIDGES ARE CLOSED...
CIVILIAN TELEGRAPH COMMUNICATION IS HALTED... TRAINS AND SHIPS HEADING SOUTH ARE DETAINED...
DOZENS OF PEOPLE ARE ARRESTED THIS NIGHT ON LITTLE OR NO EVIDENCE...
INCLUDING MISS LAURA KEENE AND THE COMPANY OF "OUR AMERICAN COUSIN."
BOOTH'S ASSOCIATES ARE SOUGHT OUT. AT SOME POINT, HIS NAME BECOMES LINKED TO THAT OF JOHN SURRATT, KNOWN TO BE A SOUTHERN COURIER.
AT ABOUT 2:00 AM, CITY DETECTIVES ARRIVE AT THE SURRATT BOARDING HOUSE IN SEARCH OF BOOTH AND JOHN SURRATT, WHO IS BELIEVED TO BE SEWARD'S ATTACKER.
LOUIS WEICHMANN EXPERIENCES A MOMENT OF REVELATION.
MY GOD... I SEE IT ALL NOW!
MRS. SURRATT EXPLAINS THAT HER SON IS IN CANADA...
AND PRODUCES A LETTER FROM HIM AS PROOF.

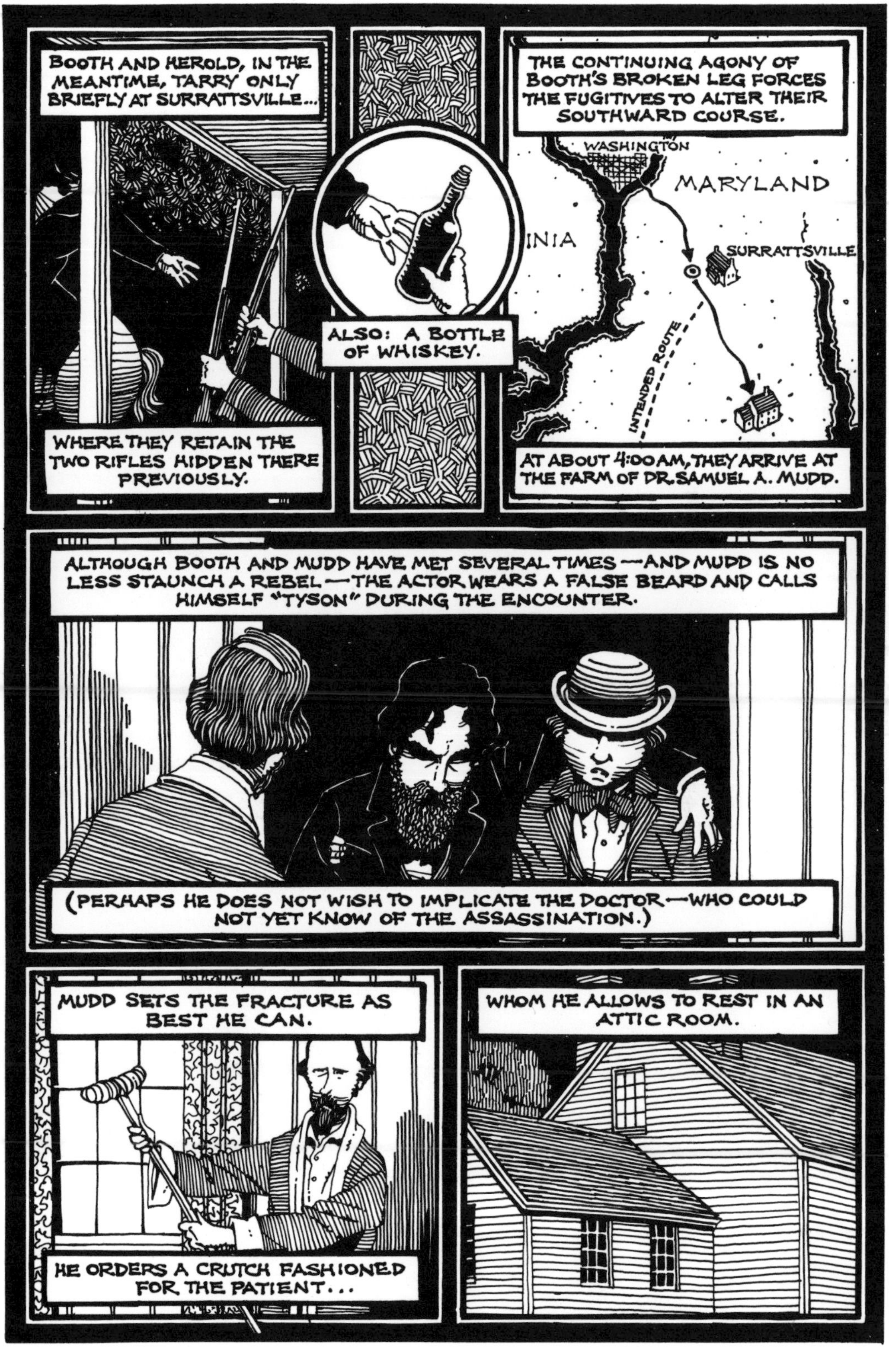
BOOTH AND HEROLD, IN THE MEANTIME, TARRY ONLY BRIEFLY AT SURRATTSVILLE...
WHERE THEY RETAIN THE TWO RIFLES HIDDEN THERE PREVIOUSLY.
ALSO: A BOTTLE OF WHISKEY.
THE CONTINUING AGONY OF BOOTH'S BROKEN LEG FORCES THE FUGITIVES TO ALTER THEIR SOUTHWARD COURSE.
WASHINGTON
MARYLAND
INIA
SURRATTSVILLE
INTENDED ROUTE
AT ABOUT 4:00 AM, THEY ARRIVE AT THE FARM OF DR. SAMUEL A. MUDD.
ALTHOUGH BOOTH AND MUDD HAVE MET SEVERAL TIMES — AND MUDD IS NO LESS STAUNCH A REBEL — THE ACTOR WEARS A FALSE BEARD AND CALLS HIMSELF "TYSON" DURING THE ENCOUNTER.
(PERHAPS HE DOES NOT WISH TO IMPLICATE THE DOCTOR — WHO COULD NOT YET KNOW OF THE ASSASSINATION.)
MUDD SETS THE FRACTURE AS BEST HE CAN.
HE ORDERS A CRUTCH FASHIONED FOR THE PATIENT...
WHOM HE ALLOWS TO REST IN AN ATTIC ROOM.

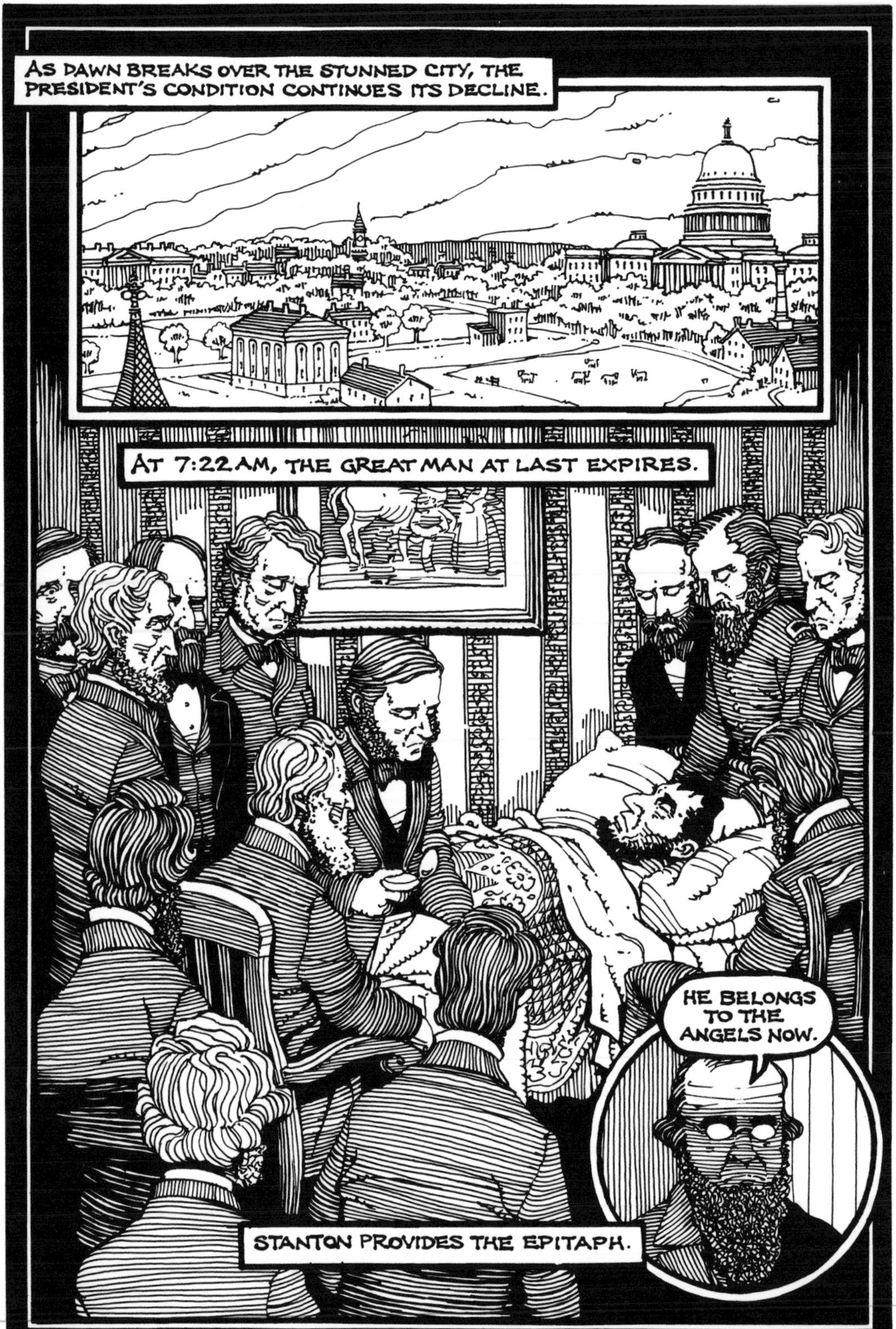
AS DAWN BREAKS OVER THE STUNNED CITY, THE PRESIDENT'S CONDITION CONTINUES ITS DECLINE.
AT 7:22AM, THE GREAT MAN AT LAST EXPIRES.
HE BELONGS TO THE ANGELS NOW.
STANTON PROVIDES THE EPITAPH.

SHORTLY AFTER LINCOLN'S DEATH IS CONFIRMED, CHIEF JUSTICE SALMON P. CHASE ARRIVES AT THE HOTEL ROOM OF VICE PRESIDENT JOHNSON...

AND SWEARS HIM IN AS PRESIDENT OF THE UNITED STATES.

A CHILLY RAIN FALLS AS THE PRESIDENT'S BODY IS BORNE BACK TO THE WHITE HOUSE.

IN A GUEST ROOM ON THE SECOND FLOOR, A PARTIAL AUTOPSY IS CONDUCTED BY THE SURGEON GENERAL, DR. JOSEPH BARNES, AND FIVE OTHERS.

THE TOP OF THE SKULL IS SAWN AWAY AND THE BRAIN REMOVED.

DURING THIS PROCEDURE THE FLATTENED BULLET IS DISLODGED, CLATTERING INTO A BASIN BELOW.

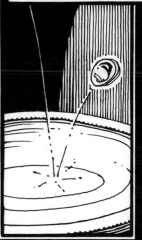

NOT LONG THEREAFTER, THE EMBALMERS GO TO WORK.

IN THE AFTERNOON, STANTON SUPERVISES THE DRESSING OF THE CORPSE, IN PREPARATION FOR A MASSIVE STATE FUNERAL.

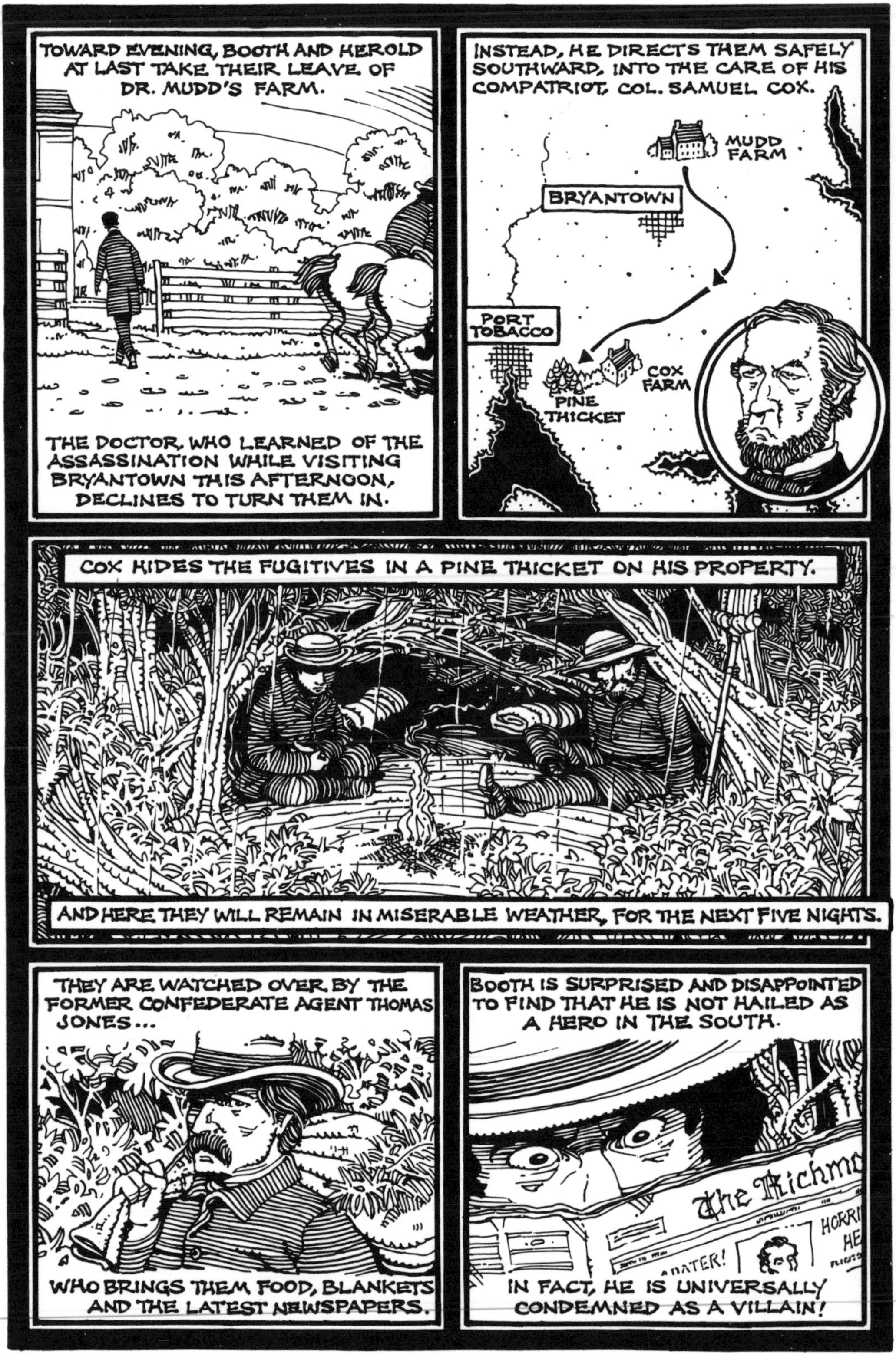
TOWARD EVENING, BOOTH AND HEROLD AT LAST TAKE THEIR LEAVE OF DR. MUDD'S FARM.
THE DOCTOR, WHO LEARNED OF THE ASSASSINATION WHILE VISITING BRYANTOWN THIS AFTERNOON, DECLINES TO TURN THEM IN.
INSTEAD, HE DIRECTS THEM SAFELY SOUTHWARD, INTO THE CARE OF HIS COMPATRIOT, COL. SAMUEL COX.
MUDD FARM
BRYANTOWN
PORT TOBACCO
COX FARM
PINE THICKET
COX HIDES THE FUGITIVES IN A PINE THICKET ON HIS PROPERTY.
AND HERE THEY WILL REMAIN IN MISERABLE WEATHER, FOR THE NEXT FIVE NIGHTS.
THEY ARE WATCHED OVER BY THE FORMER CONFEDERATE AGENT THOMAS JONES...
WHO BRINGS THEM FOOD, BLANKETS AND THE LATEST NEWSPAPERS.
BOOTH IS SURPRISED AND DISAPPOINTED TO FIND THAT HE IS NOT HAILED AS A HERO IN THE SOUTH.
The Richmo
IN FACT, HE IS UNIVERSALLY CONDEMNED AS A VILLAIN!

MONDAY, APRIL 17, 1865
ON THIS DAY, THE REMAINS OF ABRAHAM LINCOLN BEGIN THEIR PUBLIC DISPLAY. AFTER A PRIVATE VIEWING ON THE SECOND FLOOR, THE COFFIN IS MOUNTED ON A CATAFALQUE IN THE EAST ROOM.

TUESDAY, APRIL 18
THE PUBLIC STREAMS IN TO PAY ITS RESPECTS.

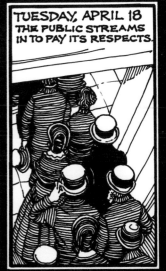

WEDNESDAY, APRIL 19, 1865
AT 12 NOON, A FUNERAL SERVICE IS CONDUCTED, AFTER WHICH THE COFFIN IS BORNE, IN A LONG, SLOW PROCESSION DOWN PENNSYLVANIA AVE. TO THE CAPITOL.

THURSDAY, APRIL 20
THE PUBLIC, IN A DOUBLE LINE OF NEVER-ENDING GRIEF, PASSES THROUGH THE GREAT ROTUNDA TO LOOK BRIEFLY UPON THE FACE OF ITS FALLEN LEADER.

FRIDAY, APRIL 21, 1865
AT 8:00 AM, IN A DREARY RAIN, THE FUNERAL TRAIN DEPARTS WASHINGTON FOR ITS LONG JOURNEY WESTWARD.

ALSO ON THE TRAIN:
THE DISINTERRED REMAINS OF THE LINCOLNS' YOUNG SON WILLIE, WHO DIED FROM TYPHOID IN 1862.

BY THIS TIME, MOST OF BOOTH'S FELLOW CONSPIRATORS HAVE BEEN TRACKED DOWN BY FEDERAL AUTHORITIES.

ON MONDAY, APRIL 17, SAMUEL ARNOLD AND MICHAEL O'LAUGHLIN ARE ARRESTED IN BALTIMORE.

ON THE SAME DAY, LEWIS POWELL, HAVING WANDERED THE STREETS OF WASHINGTON FOR THREE DAYS, AT LAST MAKES HIS WAY TO SURRATT'S BOARDING HOUSE...

ONLY TO BE TAKEN INTO CUSTODY ALONG WITH MRS. SURRATT.

THURSDAY, APRIL 20: GEORGE ATZERODT IS FOUND HIDING AMONG RELATIONS AT BARNSVILLE, MARYLAND.

ON FRIDAY, APRIL 21, DR. SAMUEL MUDD IS ARRESTED AT HIS FARM.

A REWARD OF $100,000 IS OFFERED FOR THE REMAINING FUGITIVES...

SURRAT. BOOTH. HAROLD.

War Department, Washington, April 20, 1865.

$100,000 REWARD!

THE MURDERER

(STILL WRONGLY IDENTIFYING JOHN SURRATT AS ONE OF THEM.)

AS A DETACHMENT OF CAVALRY FOLLOWS BOOTH'S TRAIL SOUTHWARD.

THE FUNERAL TRAIN, IN THE MEANTIME, PROGRESSES NORTHWARD, WITH STOPS IN BALTIMORE, HARRISBURG — AND PHILADELPHIA...

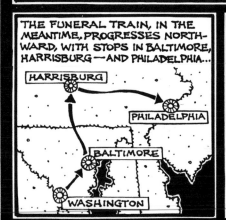

HARRISBURG

PHILADELPHIA

BALTIMORE

WASHINGTON

WHERE THE BODY LIES ON DISPLAY AT INDEPENDENCE HALL.

SATURDAY, APRIL 23 THE EAGER PUBLIC BECOMES SO TIGHTLY CROWDED THAT A RIOT ERUPTS.

ORDER IS RESTORED ONLY WITH DIFFICULTY.

FRIDAY, APRIL 21, 1865 ON THIS NIGHT, BOOTH AND HEROLD ATTEMPT TO CROSS THE POTOMAC, IN A FLAT-BOTTOMED FISHING BOAT SUPPLIED BY THOMAS JONES.

A FEDERAL GUNBOAT BLOCKS THEIR WAY DOWN-RIVER, FORCING THEM TO TURN ABOUT.

THEY END UP BACK ON THE MARYLAND SHORE, AT NANJEMOY CREEK.

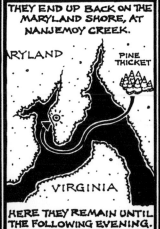

MARYLAND

PINE THICKET

VIRGINIA

HERE THEY REMAIN UNTIL THE FOLLOWING EVENING.

SAT.-SUN., APRIL 22-23 THEIR ATTEMPT TONIGHT IS SUCCESSFUL. THEY LAND AT MATHIAS POINT IN VIRGINIA.

IN THE AFTERNOON, A CONFEDERATE OPERATIVE GUIDES THEM TO THEIR SHELTER FOR THE NIGHT:

THE CABIN OF A FORMER SLAVE, WILLIAM LUCAS, HIS WIFE AND SIX CHILDREN.

THE RACIST BOOTH FORCES THE ENTIRE FAMILY TO SLEEP OUTSIDE.

MONDAY, APRIL 24, 1865 IN THE MORNING, BOOTH PAYS THE OLDEST LUCAS BOY TO TRANSPORT HEROLD AND HIMSELF, HIDDEN UNDER STRAW, IN A WAGON TO PORT CONWAY.

HERE, FATE BRINGS THE FUGITIVES INTO CONTACT WITH A TRIO OF CONFEDERATE VETERANS:

MORTIMER RUGGLES, ABSALOM BAINBRIDGE, AND WILLIAM JETT.

THE THREE SEE THEM SAFELY ACROSS THE RAPPAHANNOCK RIVER TO PORT ROYAL.

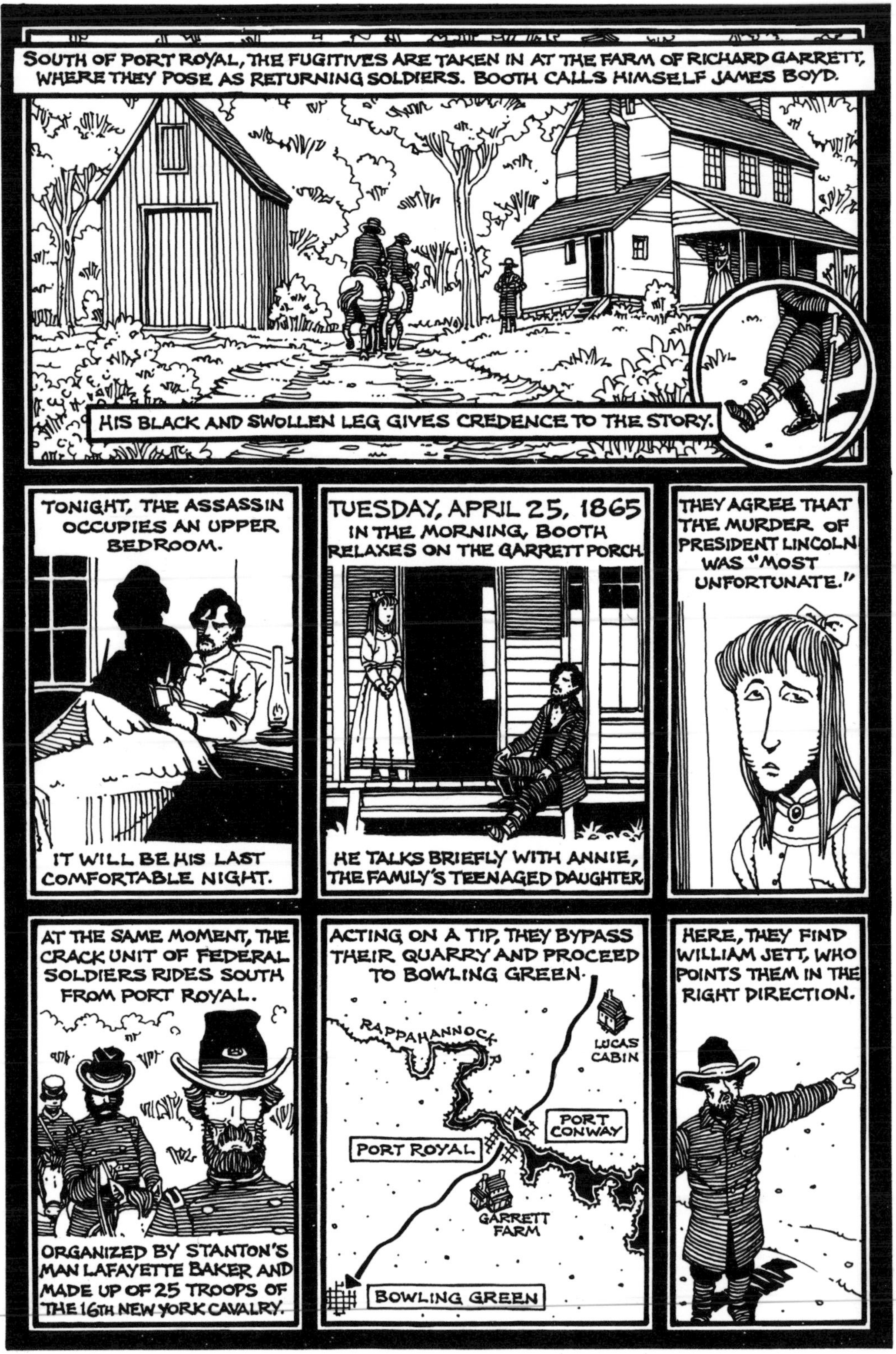

SOUTH OF PORT ROYAL, THE FUGITIVES ARE TAKEN IN AT THE FARM OF RICHARD GARRETT, WHERE THEY POSE AS RETURNING SOLDIERS. BOOTH CALLS HIMSELF JAMES BOYD.
HIS BLACK AND SWOLLEN LEG GIVES CREDENCE TO THE STORY.
TONIGHT, THE ASSASSIN OCCUPIES AN UPPER BEDROOM.
IT WILL BE HIS LAST COMFORTABLE NIGHT.
TUESDAY, APRIL 25, 1865
IN THE MORNING, BOOTH RELAXES ON THE GARRETT PORCH.
HE TALKS BRIEFLY WITH ANNIE, THE FAMILY'S TEENAGED DAUGHTER.
THEY AGREE THAT THE MURDER OF PRESIDENT LINCOLN WAS "MOST UNFORTUNATE."
AT THE SAME MOMENT, THE CRACK UNIT OF FEDERAL SOLDIERS RIDES SOUTH FROM PORT ROYAL.
ORGANIZED BY STANTON'S MAN LAFAYETTE BAKER AND MADE UP OF 25 TROOPS OF THE 16TH NEW YORK CAVALRY.
ACTING ON A TIP, THEY BYPASS THEIR QUARRY AND PROCEED TO BOWLING GREEN.
RAPPAHANNOCK R.
LUCAS CABIN
PORT CONWAY
PORT ROYAL
GARRETT FARM
BOWLING GREEN
HERE, THEY FIND WILLIAM JETT, WHO POINTS THEM IN THE RIGHT DIRECTION.

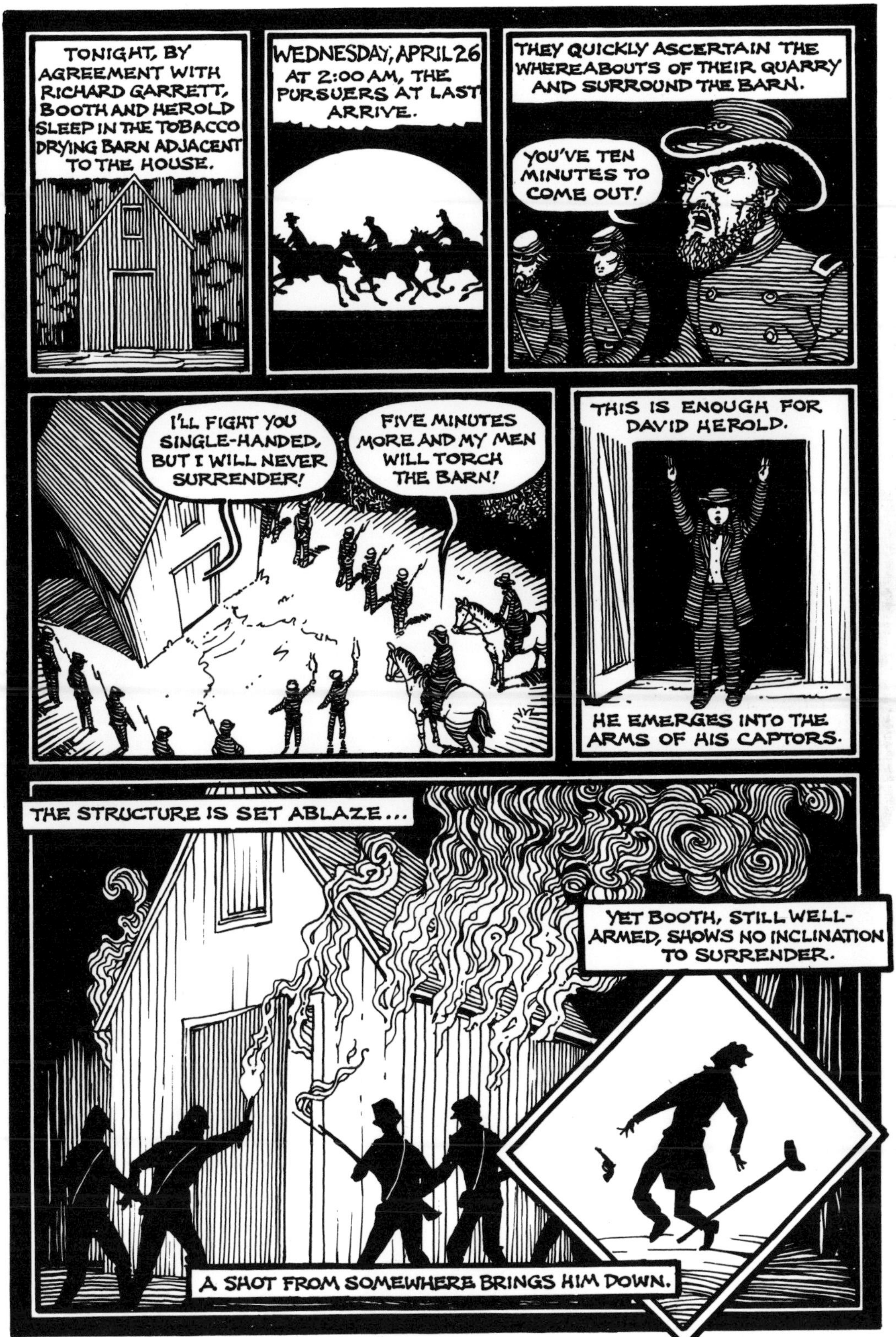
TONIGHT, BY AGREEMENT WITH RICHARD GARRETT, BOOTH AND HEROLD SLEEP IN THE TOBACCO DRYING BARN ADJACENT TO THE HOUSE.
WEDNESDAY, APRIL 26 AT 2:00 AM, THE PURSUERS AT LAST ARRIVE.
THEY QUICKLY ASCERTAIN THE WHEREABOUTS OF THEIR QUARRY AND SURROUND THE BARN.
YOU'VE TEN MINUTES TO COME OUT!
I'LL FIGHT YOU SINGLE-HANDED, BUT I WILL NEVER SURRENDER!
FIVE MINUTES MORE AND MY MEN WILL TORCH THE BARN!
THIS IS ENOUGH FOR DAVID HEROLD.
HE EMERGES INTO THE ARMS OF HIS CAPTORS.
THE STRUCTURE IS SET ABLAZE...
YET BOOTH, STILL WELL-ARMED, SHOWS NO INCLINATION TO SURRENDER.
A SHOT FROM SOMEWHERE BRINGS HIM DOWN.

THE DYING ASSASSIN IS DRAGGED FROM THE BARN TO THE GARRETTS' PORCH.

A SARGEANT NAMED BOSTON CORBETT CLAIMS CREDIT FOR THE SHOT — ACTING, HE SAYS, UNDER A COMMAND FROM GOD.

SOME ARE LEFT TO WONDER, HOWEVER, IF BOOTH COMMITTED THE DEED HIMSELF.

THE ACTOR CLINGS TO CONSCIOUSNESS FOR A FEW MINUTES LONGER.

TELL MY MOTHER THAT I DIE FOR MY COUNTRY...

I DID WHAT I THOUGHT WAS BEST...

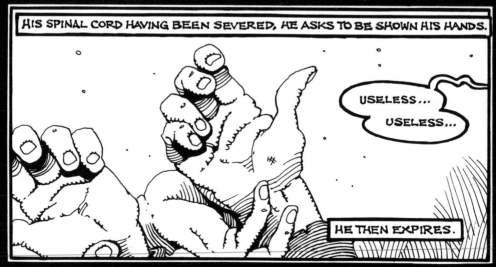

HIS SPINAL CORD HAVING BEEN SEVERED, HE ASKS TO BE SHOWN HIS HANDS.

USELESS...

USELESS...

HE THEN EXPIRES.

PART V.
LAID TO REST

FUNERAL CARRIAGE

MONDAY, APRIL 24, 1865
AS ABRAHAM LINCOLN'S MURDERER IS HUNTED DOWN, THE FUNERAL TRAIN CONTINUES ITS PROGRESS: FROM PHILADELPHIA, THROUGH TRENTON, TO JERSEY CITY.

FROM HERE, THE COFFIN IS FERRIED ACROSS THE HUDSON RIVER TO NEW YORK CITY.

A SLOW, SAD PROCESSION BRINGS IT DOWN BROADWAY TO THE CITY HALL,...

WHERE IT LIES ON DISPLAY IN THE GREAT ROTUNDA.

BEFORE THE PUBLIC IS ALLOWED INSIDE, AN ENTERPRISING PHOTOGRAPHER TAKES AN IMAGE OF THE CORPSE.

BUT, UNDER ORDERS FROM EDWIN M. STANTON, THE PLATES ARE SEIZED AND DESTROYED.

TUESDAY, APRIL 25
AT 2:00 PM, ANOTHER PROCESSION MAKES ITS WAY TO THE RAIL DEPOT AT 9TH AVENUE AND 34TH ST.

THE TRAIN DEPARTS NORTHWARD FOR ALBANY (WITH STOPS AT WEST POINT AND POUGHKEEPSIE)

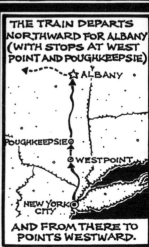

ALBANY

POUGHKEEPSIE

WESTPOINT

NEW YORK CITY

AND FROM THERE TO POINTS WESTWARD.

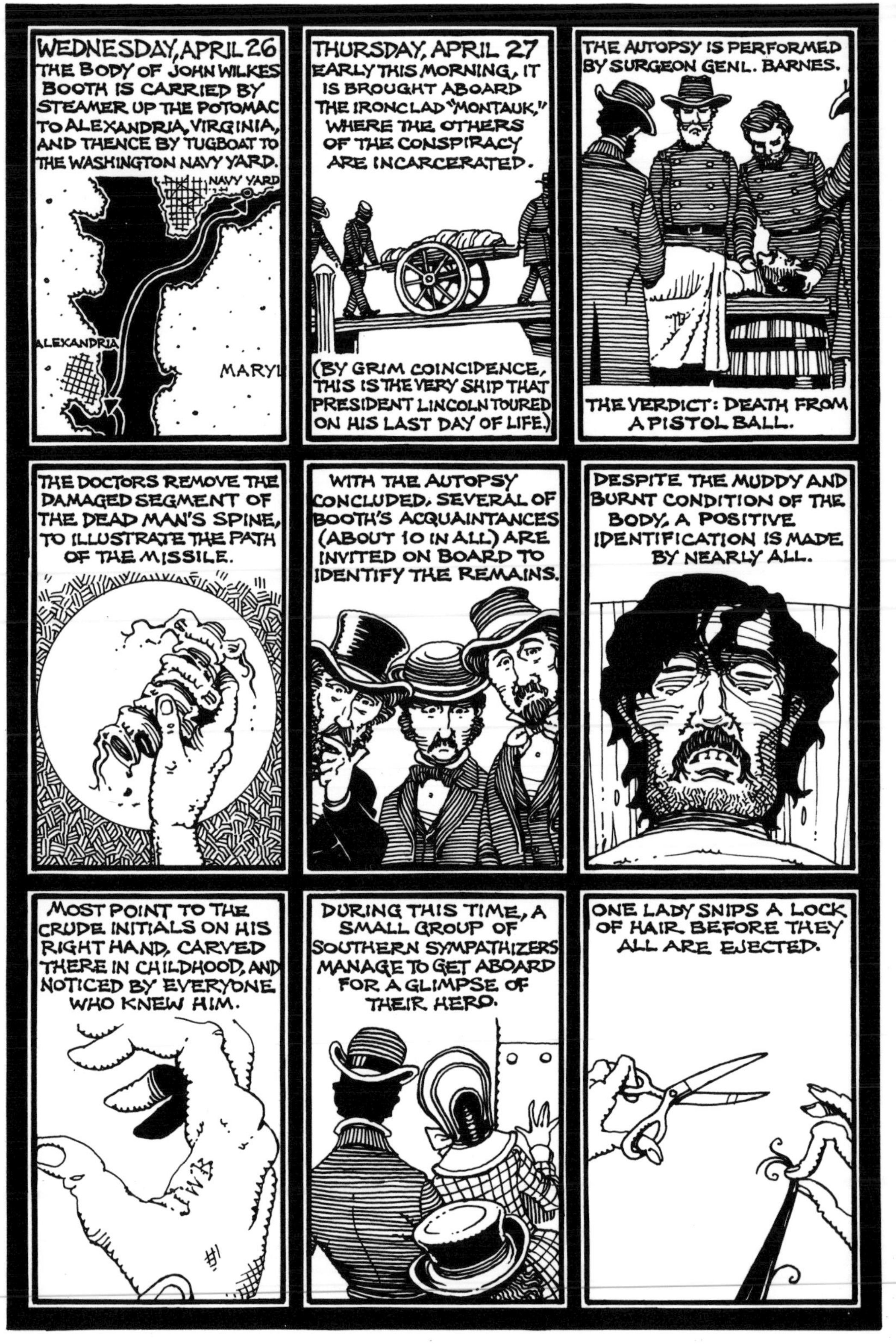
WEDNESDAY, APRIL 26
THE BODY OF JOHN WILKES BOOTH IS CARRIED BY STEAMER UP THE POTOMAC TO ALEXANDRIA, VIRGINIA, AND THENCE BY TUGBOAT TO THE WASHINGTON NAVY YARD.
NAVY YARD
ALEXANDRIA
MARYL
THURSDAY, APRIL 27
EARLY THIS MORNING, IT IS BROUGHT ABOARD THE IRONCLAD "MONTAUK," WHERE THE OTHERS OF THE CONSPIRACY ARE INCARCERATED.
(BY GRIM COINCIDENCE, THIS IS THE VERY SHIP THAT PRESIDENT LINCOLN TOURED ON HIS LAST DAY OF LIFE.)
THE AUTOPSY IS PERFORMED BY SURGEON GENL. BARNES.
THE VERDICT: DEATH FROM A PISTOL BALL.
THE DOCTORS REMOVE THE DAMAGED SEGMENT OF THE DEAD MAN'S SPINE, TO ILLUSTRATE THE PATH OF THE MISSILE.
WITH THE AUTOPSY CONCLUDED, SEVERAL OF BOOTH'S ACQUAINTANCES (ABOUT 10 IN ALL) ARE INVITED ON BOARD TO IDENTIFY THE REMAINS.
DESPITE THE MUDDY AND BURNT CONDITION OF THE BODY, A POSITIVE IDENTIFICATION IS MADE BY NEARLY ALL.
MOST POINT TO THE CRUDE INITIALS ON HIS RIGHT HAND, CARVED THERE IN CHILDHOOD, AND NOTICED BY EVERYONE WHO KNEW HIM.
JWB
DURING THIS TIME, A SMALL GROUP OF SOUTHERN SYMPATHIZERS MANAGE TO GET ABOARD FOR A GLIMPSE OF THEIR HERO.
ONE LADY SNIPS A LOCK OF HAIR BEFORE THEY ALL ARE EJECTED.

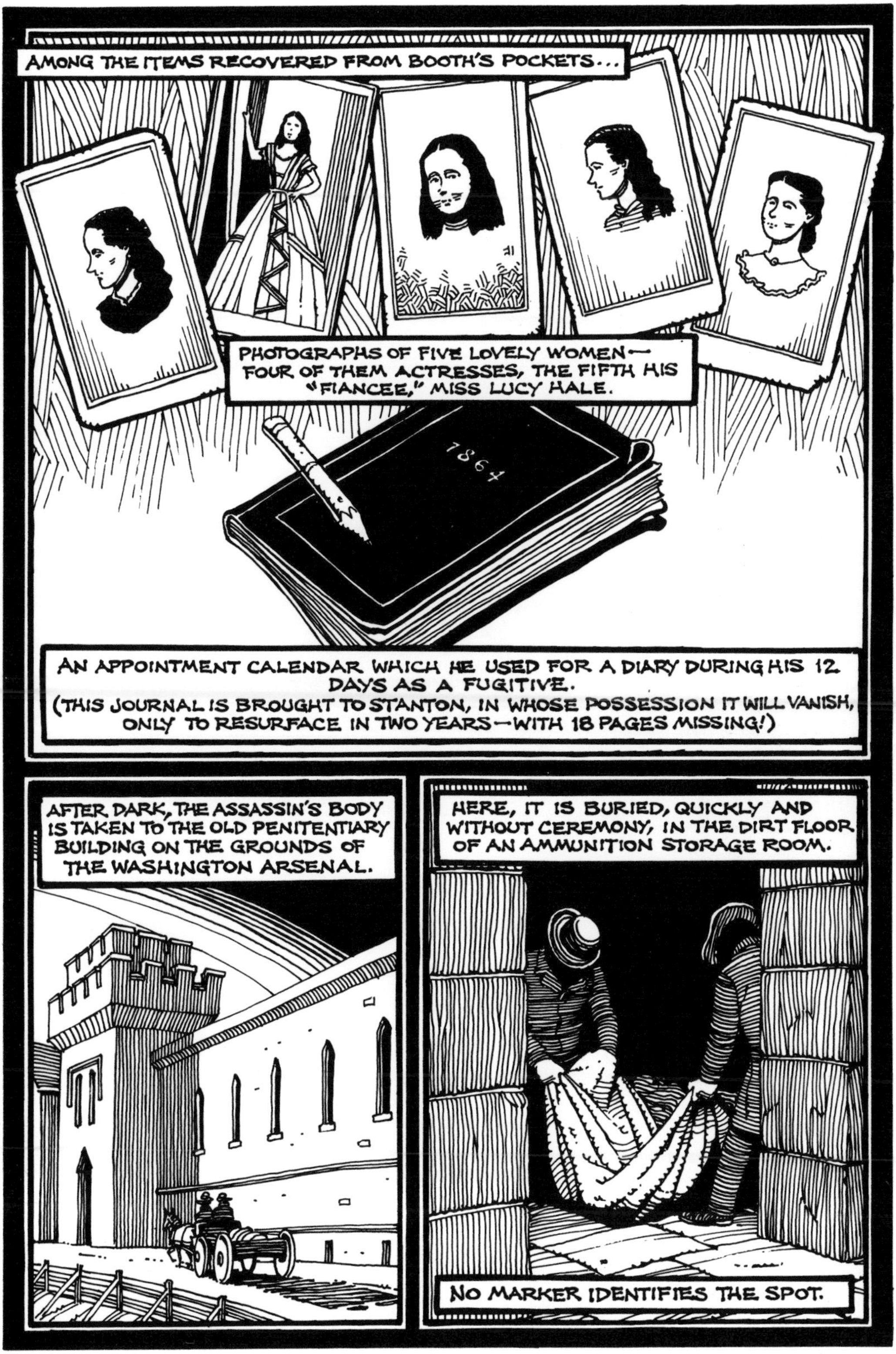

AMONG THE ITEMS RECOVERED FROM BOOTH'S POCKETS...
PHOTOGRAPHS OF FIVE LOVELY WOMEN— FOUR OF THEM ACTRESSES, THE FIFTH HIS "FIANCEE," MISS LUCY HALE.
1864
AN APPOINTMENT CALENDAR WHICH HE USED FOR A DIARY DURING HIS 12 DAYS AS A FUGITIVE. (THIS JOURNAL IS BROUGHT TO STANTON, IN WHOSE POSSESSION IT WILL VANISH, ONLY TO RESURFACE IN TWO YEARS—WITH 18 PAGES MISSING!)
AFTER DARK, THE ASSASSIN'S BODY IS TAKEN TO THE OLD PENITENTIARY BUILDING ON THE GROUNDS OF THE WASHINGTON ARSENAL.
HERE, IT IS BURIED, QUICKLY AND WITHOUT CEREMONY, IN THE DIRT FLOOR OF AN AMMUNITION STORAGE ROOM.
NO MARKER IDENTIFIES THE SPOT.

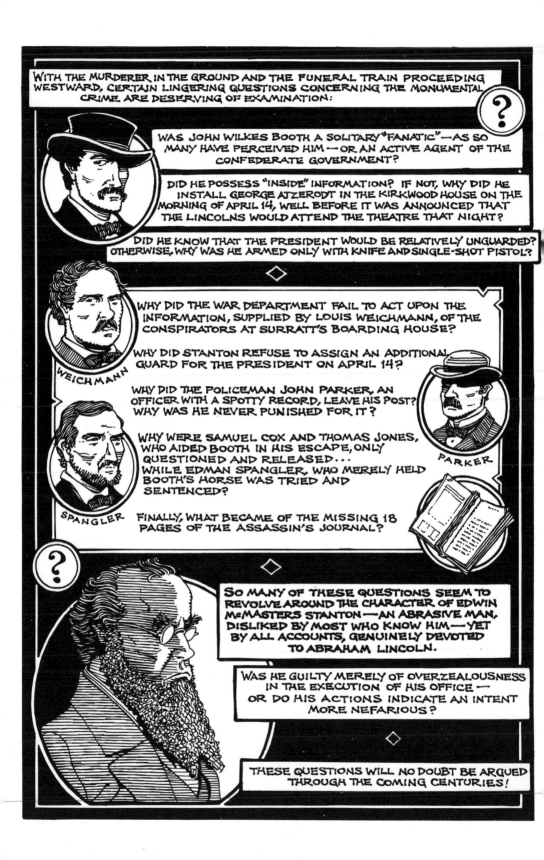

WITH THE MURDERER IN THE GROUND AND THE FUNERAL TRAIN PROCEEDING WESTWARD, CERTAIN LINGERING QUESTIONS CONCERNING THE MONUMENTAL CRIME ARE DESERVING OF EXAMINATION:

WAS JOHN WILKES BOOTH A SOLITARY "FANATIC"—AS SO MANY HAVE PERCEIVED HIM—OR AN ACTIVE AGENT OF THE CONFEDERATE GOVERNMENT?

DID HE POSSESS "INSIDE" INFORMATION? IF NOT, WHY DID HE INSTALL GEORGE ATZERODT IN THE KIRKWOOD HOUSE ON THE MORNING OF APRIL 14, WELL BEFORE IT WAS ANNOUNCED THAT THE LINCOLNS WOULD ATTEND THE THEATRE THAT NIGHT?

DID HE KNOW THAT THE PRESIDENT WOULD BE RELATIVELY UNGUARDED? OTHERWISE, WHY WAS HE ARMED ONLY WITH KNIFE AND SINGLE-SHOT PISTOL?

WHY DID THE WAR DEPARTMENT FAIL TO ACT UPON THE INFORMATION, SUPPLIED BY LOUIS WEICHMANN, OF THE CONSPIRATORS AT SURRATT'S BOARDING HOUSE?

WEICHMANN

WHY DID STANTON REFUSE TO ASSIGN AN ADDITIONAL GUARD FOR THE PRESIDENT ON APRIL 14?

WHY DID THE POLICEMAN JOHN PARKER, AN OFFICER WITH A SPOTTY RECORD, LEAVE HIS POST? WHY WAS HE NEVER PUNISHED FOR IT?

WHY WERE SAMUEL COX AND THOMAS JONES, WHO AIDED BOOTH IN HIS ESCAPE, ONLY QUESTIONED AND RELEASED... WHILE EDMAN SPANGLER, WHO MERELY HELD BOOTH'S HORSE WAS TRIED AND SENTENCED?

PARKER

SPANGLER

FINALLY, WHAT BECAME OF THE MISSING 18 PAGES OF THE ASSASSIN'S JOURNAL?

SO MANY OF THESE QUESTIONS SEEM TO REVOLVE AROUND THE CHARACTER OF EDWIN McMASTERS STANTON—AN ABRASIVE MAN, DISLIKED BY MOST WHO KNOW HIM—YET BY ALL ACCOUNTS, GENUINELY DEVOTED TO ABRAHAM LINCOLN.

WAS HE GUILTY MERELY OF OVERZEALOUSNESS IN THE EXECUTION OF HIS OFFICE— OR DO HIS ACTIONS INDICATE AN INTENT MORE NEFARIOUS?

THESE QUESTIONS WILL NO DOUBT BE ARGUED THROUGH THE COMING CENTURIES!

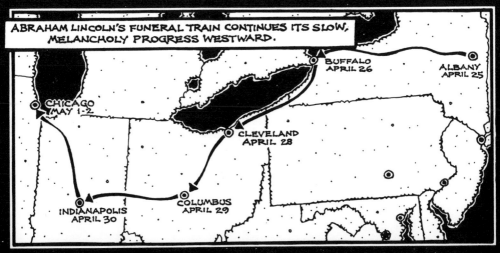

ABRAHAM LINCOLN'S FUNERAL TRAIN CONTINUES ITS SLOW, MELANCHOLY PROGRESS WESTWARD.

BUFFALO APRIL 26

ALBANY APRIL 25

CHICAGO MAY 1-2

CLEVELAND APRIL 28

INDIANAPOLIS APRIL 30

COLUMBUS APRIL 29

AT EACH STOP, GREAT THRONGS BRAVE DRENCHING RAINS TO PAY TRIBUTE.

MONDAY, MAY 1, 1865 AT 11:00 AM, THE TRAIN ARRIVES AT CHICAGO, FOR A SOLEMN PROCESSION THROUGH THE CITY...

ACE, NOBLE SOUL, PAT

AND DISPLAY OF THE REMAINS AT THE COOK COUNTY COURT HOUSE.

THE PUBLIC FILES BY THROUGH THE NIGHT AND INTO THE FOLLOWING AFTERNOON.

TUESDAY, MAY 2 AT 9:30 PM, THE TRAIN LEAVES CHICAGO ON THE FINAL SEGMENT OF ITS SORROWFUL JOURNEY.

CHICAGO

SPRINGFIELD

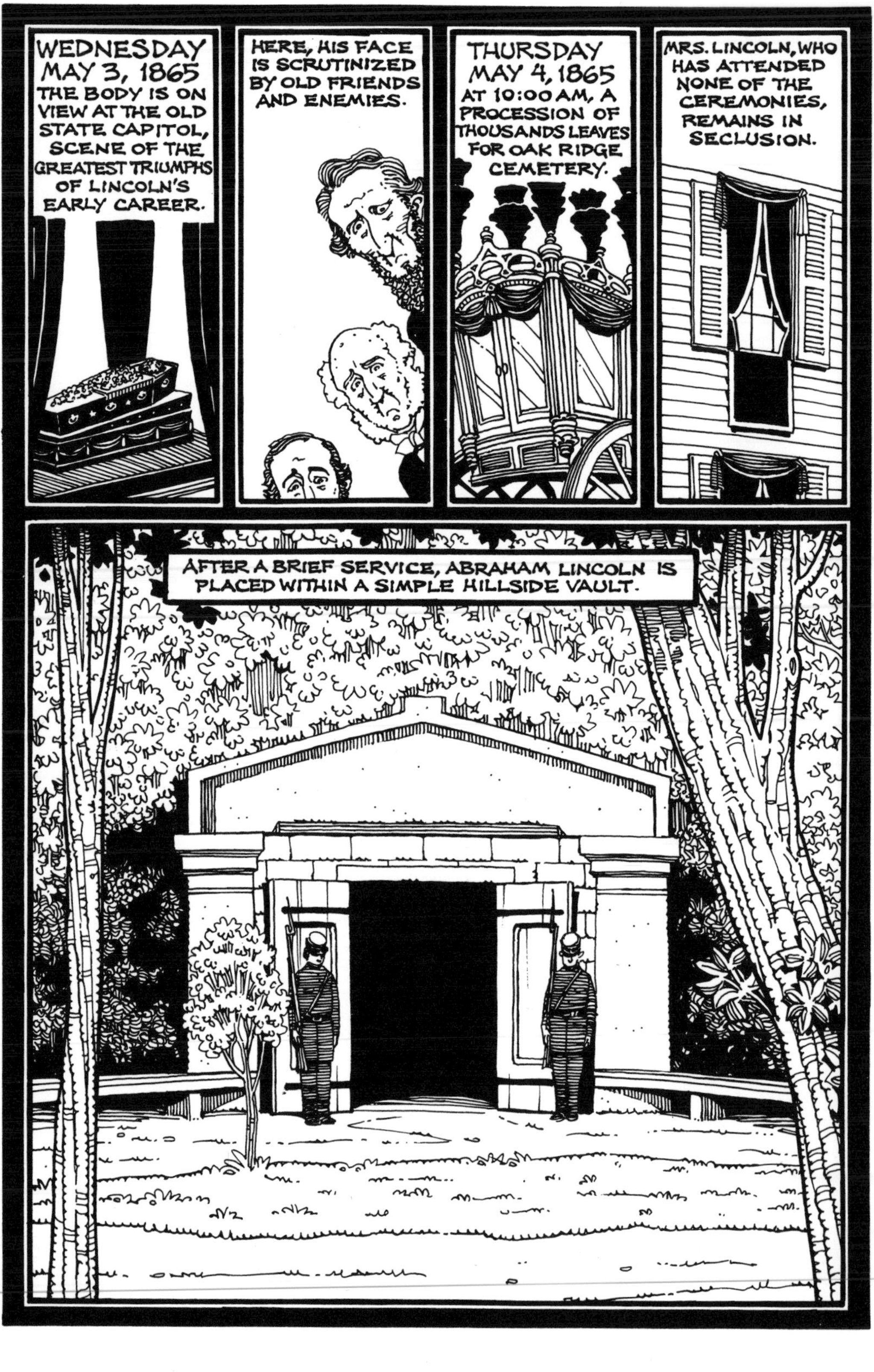
WEDNESDAY MAY 3, 1865
THE BODY IS ON VIEW AT THE OLD STATE CAPITOL, SCENE OF THE GREATEST TRIUMPHS OF LINCOLN'S EARLY CAREER.
HERE, HIS FACE IS SCRUTINIZED BY OLD FRIENDS AND ENEMIES.
THURSDAY MAY 4, 1865
AT 10:00 AM, A PROCESSION OF THOUSANDS LEAVES FOR OAK RIDGE CEMETERY.
MRS. LINCOLN, WHO HAS ATTENDED NONE OF THE CEREMONIES, REMAINS IN SECLUSION.
AFTER A BRIEF SERVICE, ABRAHAM LINCOLN IS PLACED WITHIN A SIMPLE HILLSIDE VAULT.

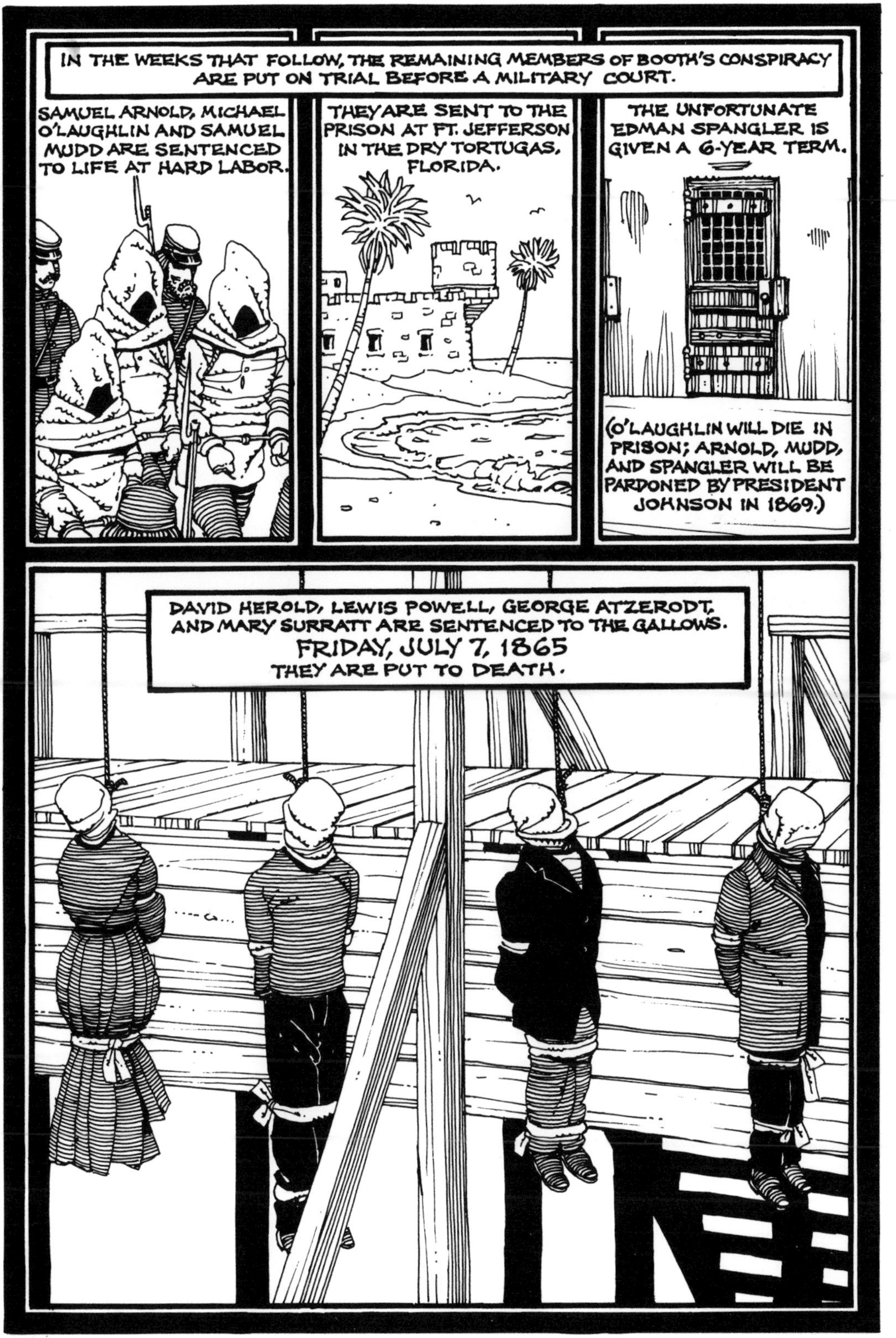
IN THE WEEKS THAT FOLLOW, THE REMAINING MEMBERS OF BOOTH'S CONSPIRACY ARE PUT ON TRIAL BEFORE A MILITARY COURT.
SAMUEL ARNOLD, MICHAEL O'LAUGHLIN AND SAMUEL MUDD ARE SENTENCED TO LIFE AT HARD LABOR.
THEY ARE SENT TO THE PRISON AT FT. JEFFERSON IN THE DRY TORTUGAS, FLORIDA.
THE UNFORTUNATE EDMAN SPANGLER IS GIVEN A 6-YEAR TERM.
(O'LAUGHLIN WILL DIE IN PRISON; ARNOLD, MUDD, AND SPANGLER WILL BE PARDONED BY PRESIDENT JOHNSON IN 1869.)
DAVID HEROLD, LEWIS POWELL, GEORGE ATZERODT, AND MARY SURRATT ARE SENTENCED TO THE GALLOWS.
FRIDAY, JULY 7, 1865
THEY ARE PUT TO DEATH.

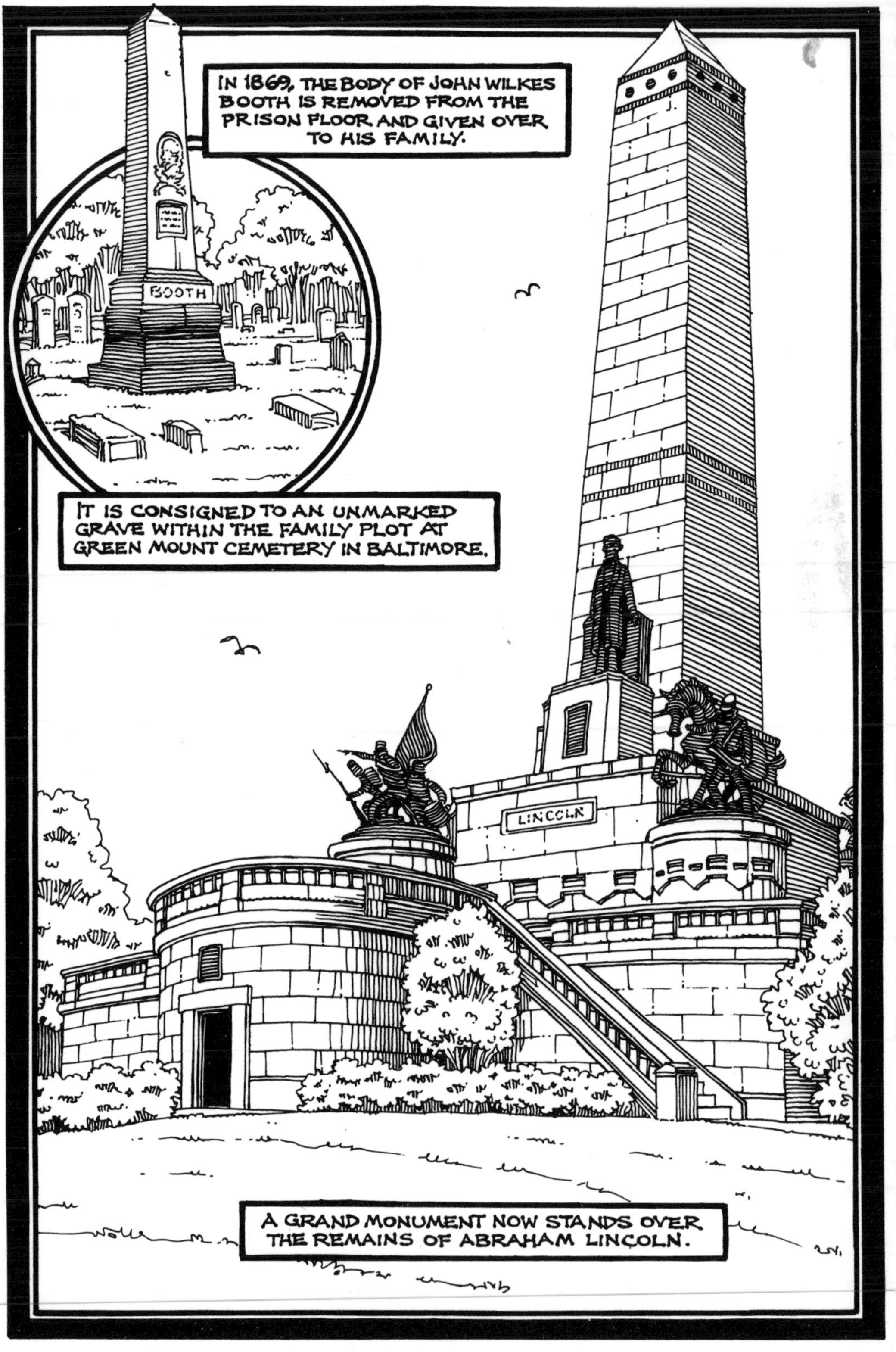
IN 1869, THE BODY OF JOHN WILKES BOOTH IS REMOVED FROM THE PRISON FLOOR AND GIVEN OVER TO HIS FAMILY.
BOOTH
IT IS CONSIGNED TO AN UNMARKED GRAVE WITHIN THE FAMILY PLOT AT GREEN MOUNT CEMETERY IN BALTIMORE.
LINCOLN
A GRAND MONUMENT NOW STANDS OVER THE REMAINS OF ABRAHAM LINCOLN.